What Goes Around

Belts by Lois Ericson

To my father who taught me to be a dreamer

Credits

Special thanks: To Bets Barnard for her assistance and expertise in the editing department. To my life's partner, Len for his encouragement and support.

Sewing assistance:
Nancy Grimshaw
Betty Worral
Proofreading:
Jane Lamb
Margaret Scoville

Eric's PRESS

Contents

Introduction

Belts are an outstanding fashion accessory. Fast and easy to make, either for yourself, for gifts or for sale. It is a short term project that requires very little material. Any technique and embellishment can be utilized to create a belt. The style of it can be casual and utilitarian to elegant and frivolous. Almost anyone can wear a belt. If you are not happy with the size of your waist, I suggest wearing the belt under an open jacket or vest to create the illusion of a waistline (no one will know the exact size).

It is quite amazing how easily the look of an old favorite garment in your wardrobe can be transformed by several new belts. Think about it -- instead of making many new garments -- make some new belts. This is an especially good idea for the women who work away from home and have to dress up every day, with little time to sew. A belt can be made in an hour or two. (You get faster after you've make a couple.)

Color is a definite factor in the belt success 'story'. It creates the mood. The belt can match an outfit, contrast to emphasize your best feature, or echo the hue of jewelry or scarf. The following pages are filled with ideas to inspire and motivate you to add a new look to your belt wardrobe.

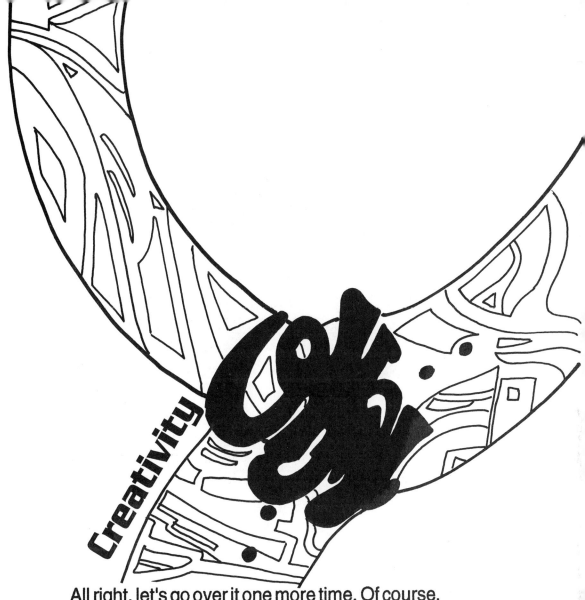

Creativity

COPY

All right, let's go over it one more time. Of course, you are creative! How do we find the inspiration? The same way we get inspired to do any creative project. COPY! Just kidding! It's o.k. to copy to learn the process -- but after you 'get it' -- put your own stamp of individuality on your work. This book will show you a variety of belts and maybe at least one or two of the ideas will get you started.

The Basics

The choice of a belt is a very important one to create the total look. It will add interest and coordinate your outfit. There are an unlimited number of choices -- in every shape, color, material and design. I use a variety of fabrics for belts, any fabric can be usable. Firm fabrics might be a good choice since they are easy to work with ... i.e. corduroy, cotton, denim, suiting. However, even the softest or sheerest materials can be used successfully if interfaced properly. The color is my first consideration, then I figure out how to make the fabric work as a belt. In addition to fabric, other materials to consider, might be leather, Ultrasuede, cording/rope, or elastic in various widths.

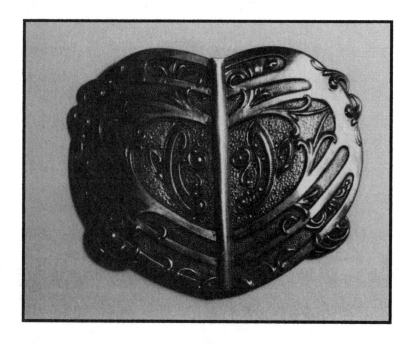

The belt could be very plain and straightforward, with an incredible buckle on it. The exquisite fabric could be the main feature. The texture could be superb! Even the shape of the belt could be the most exciting part.

Will it buckle, tie, button or ? Bracelets can be easily used to fasten a belt. The round ones can be fastened on with a tab of fabric, then tied with a band of fabric at the other end of the belt. If the bracelet or necklace is a link-type, maybe the fastener can hold the belt together and the remaining links can be decorative.

The first decision is the size -- width and length of the belt. I find that most people are more creative if they rely on themselves to make the pattern. It's easy. Cut a piece of fabric approximately the size of the finished belt, considering the overlap. Wrap it around your waist or hips and look in the mirror. Add or subtract where necessary to make the shape flattering for your body. Congratulations! You've just made a pattern.

If a belt is to be straight, it has to be narrow to fit the waist. We all curve in the middle (to varying degrees).

Alternatives to make a straight but wide belt work:

...... fasten at an angle. Experiment with a straight piece of fabric. Place the ties where appropriate.

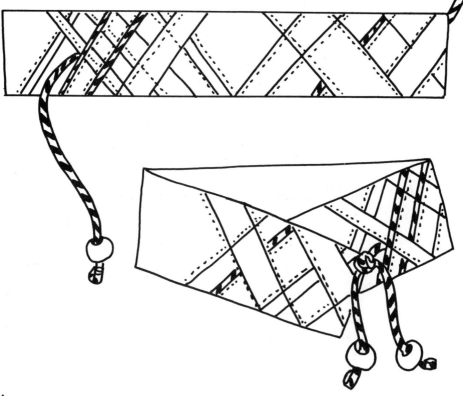

.... make darts, in the pattern, to nip in the waist slightly to fit the curve. Cut the fabric and interfacing as the curved shape, without the darts.

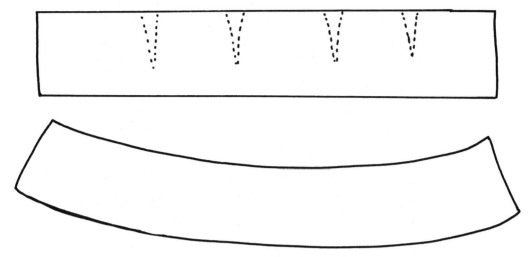

..... place a 30" tie at each end of a straight belt. Make a buttonhole 3 - 5" from one end of the straight belt. To fasten, wrap around and slide tie thru buttonhole.

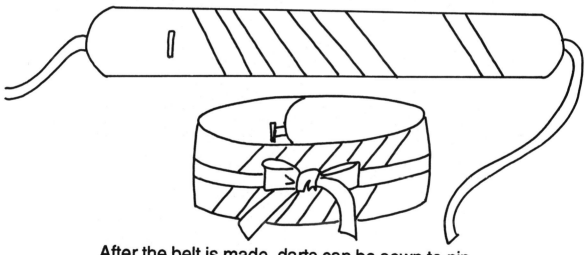

After the belt is made, darts can be sewn to nip in the waist, as desired. For this idea, you could also start with a straight piece of fabric.

After the basic shape has been decided, cut out an interfacing using the 'pattern' just made. There are many choices for the interfacing, most often a very firm one is best. One that I especially like is called Fuse-A-Shade (used to make window shades). When the choice is an iron-on, I fuse it to a tightly woven cotton. If I'm making several belts I prepare my interfacing/cotton fabric in a one yard piece the whole width of the fabric. Now I can cut out several belt shapes, speeding up my preparation time.

Another choice for interfacing would be a woven or lightweight iron-on for a soft,wrap belt. If an iron-on is used I recommend ironing it onto the lining side, I don't usually fuse it to my fashion fabric. If the belt is to have a quilted look, the belt shape can be cut out of a lightweight batting such as Thermore or Cotton Classic or a 'generic' similar to these. If the belt is to be stiff -- lightweight canvas works well. Commercial belting, available in several widths, is recommended for a straight firm belt.

The next step is to cover the interfacing with the fabrics chosen.Stitching the fashion fabric directly to the interfacing will keep all layers in place. I recommend extending the fabrics about 1/2" all around, beyond the edges of the interfacing. Cut the lining larger too. When the belt is sewn together the stiff interfacing isn't included in the seam.... less bulk.

When the belt is a series of pieces, I stitch them directly onto the interfacing, with the 1/2" extensions as mentioned on the previous page.

When covering the interfacing with the fabric, a technique to make the surface interesting is a consideration. Many are suggested in this book, as well as in other books I have written over the years. By combining these ideas with the skills you already have, you have a wealth of information at your disposal.

When attaching the lining, place the right side of the lining facing the right side of the belt. Pin in place. If there are ties or other fastening devices to be included in the seams, this is the time to pin them in the appropriate places, so they are included in the seams. Usually I stitch both ends and the top edges of the belt with the lining, leaving most of the bottom edge open... to make it easy to turn to the other right side. Depending on the embellishment on the belt, it is easier to hand tack the bottom edge than it is to turn the belt thru a small opening. Note: this style of belt can be worn with the point facing up or down.

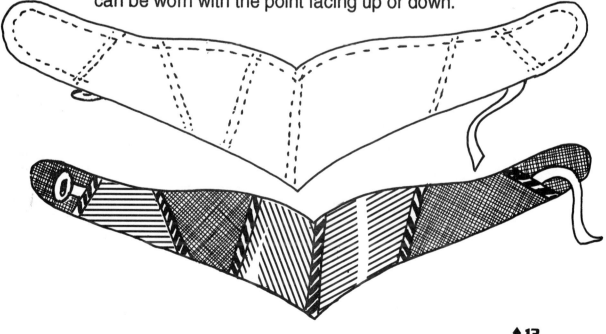

If the shape of the outer edge of the belt is very intricate, see diagram below for an excellent way to attach the lining.

Make a paper pattern of the belt. Cut the pattern in two, lengthwise. Add 2" to the the center cut. Cut lining, same as pattern with the additional 2". Press 1" of the additional 2".Overlap 1" and baste the center 'line' together. Place the lining on the belt, right sides together. Pin at the outer edges leaving the overlap open. Stitch, trim and clip seams, all around. Remove basting. Turn to right side thru overlapped opening. Hand sew overlap closed.

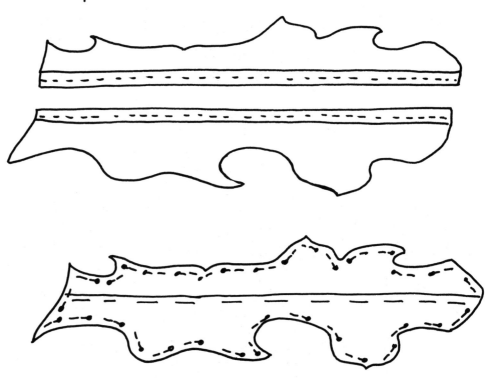

TIE ONE ON!

Sashes can be twisted & knotted to add color and texture. Make an extra long necktie, for the waist and tie it like a tie! A narrow belt on top of a wide belt or cumberbund can be interesting. For a casual look wear two very narrow belts together. Consider wearing a narrow (purchased) leather belt with one you've made -- Hey I'm not a purist! Look in the men's department for belts and suspenders. (Fashion trick for women: wear men's suspenders backwards so the 'Y' is in the front.)

Belts for daytime are usually narrow, that's why the loops are there on pants and skirts. The fabric and embellishment would be the main consideration for a daytime or evening belt. For evening a wide flashy belt would be a great addition to your wardrobe.

Gallery

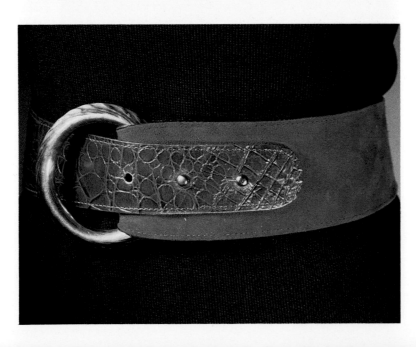

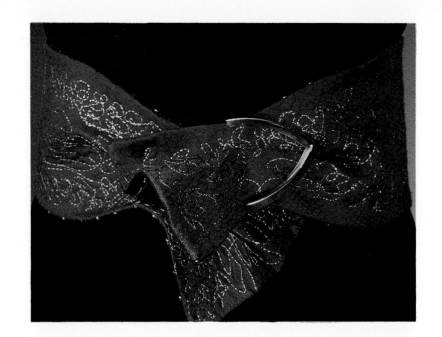

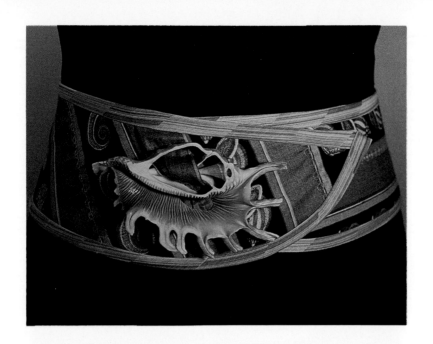

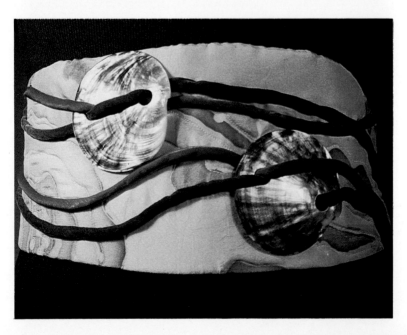

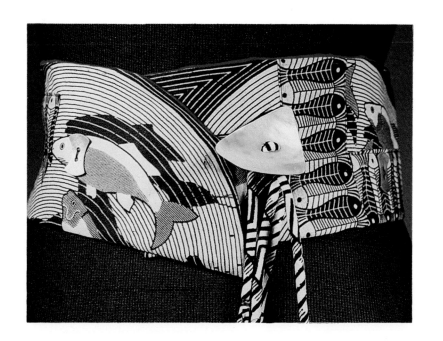

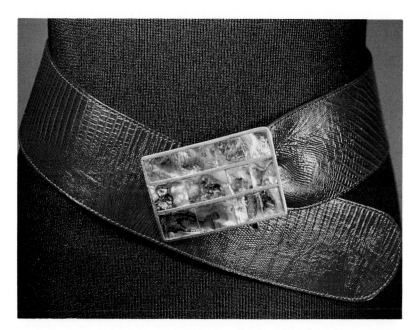

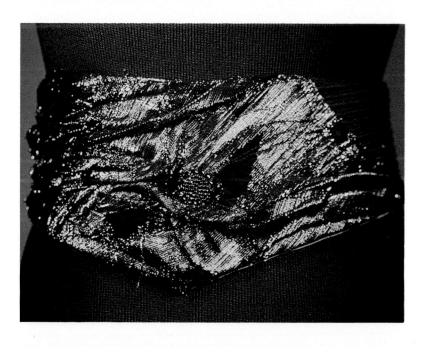

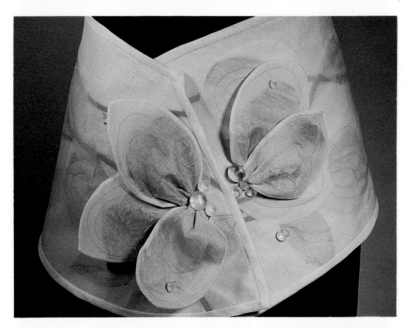

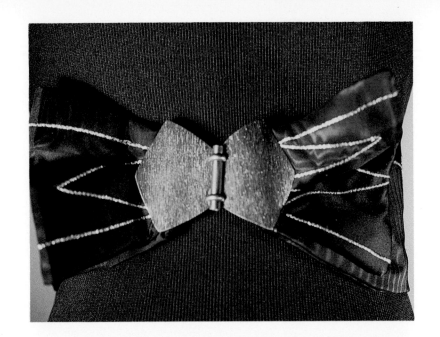

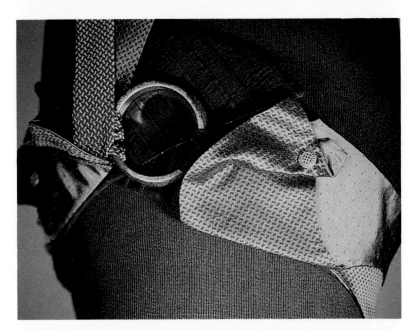

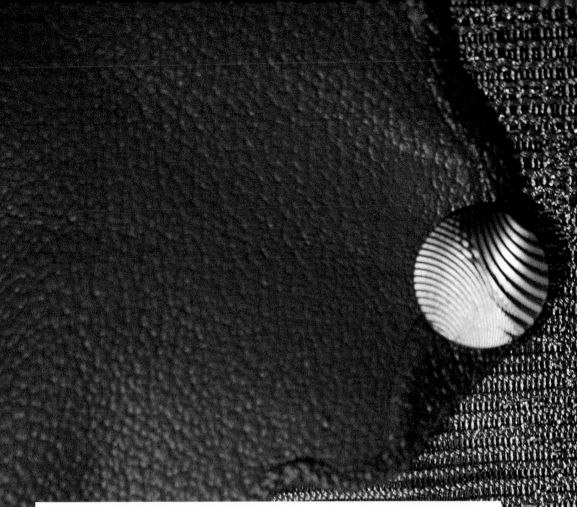

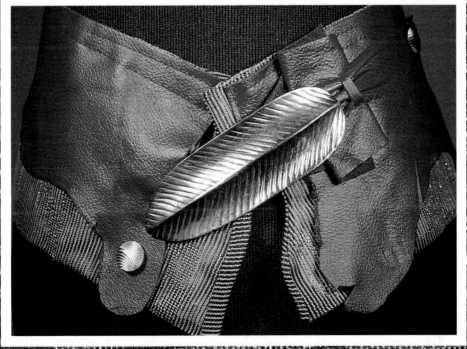

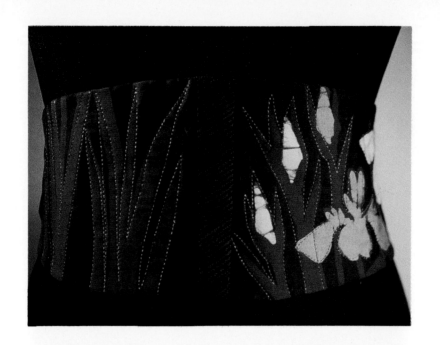

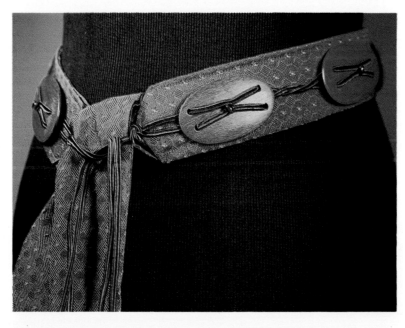

Closures

Closure relates to the ending or conclusion. The closure, in the case of a belt, may be the beginning. Many of the decisions in the beginning or design stage of making a belt, have to do with the ending.

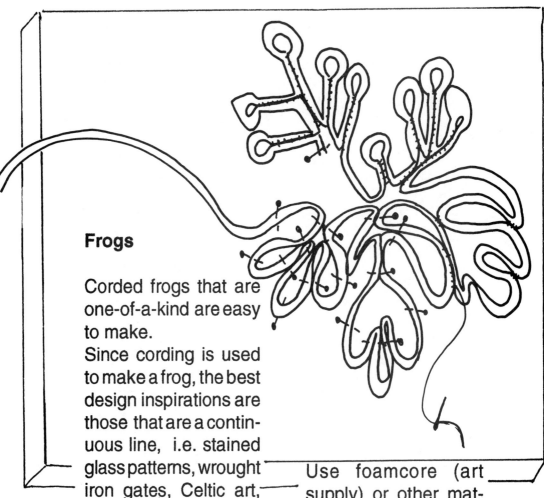

Frogs

Corded frogs that are one-of-a-kind are easy to make.

Since cording is used to make a frog, the best design inspirations are those that are a continuous line, i.e. stained glass patterns, wrought iron gates, Celtic art, Indian designs, calligraphy. Contour drawings would be perfect because they too are a continous line, as is the cording. There is a variety of cording available in fabric stores, or you may choose to make your own.

Use foamcore (art supply) or other material that you can pin to for a 'board'. Pin one end of the cording to the foamcore. Continue turning, curving, looping the cord to make the design, pinning to the board, as you position the cord. Overcast the cording, hand stitch where the cord meets. The stitches won't show because the 'wrong' side is up. Note: one of the loops can be a buttonhole.

Thanks to Diane Ericson for this idea.

POSSIBILITIES:

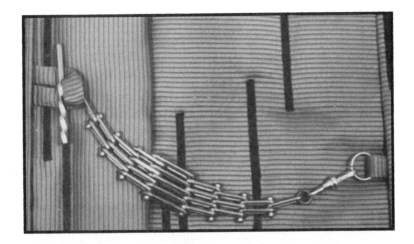

watch chain

antique book hinge fastens to a brass button

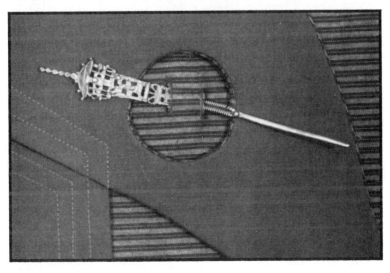

oriental hair ornament

POSSIBILITIES:

BRACELETS

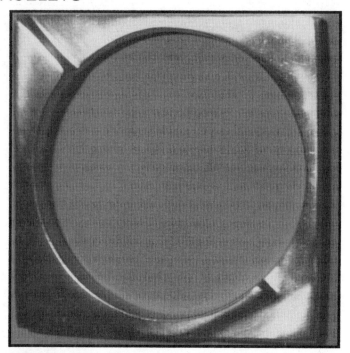

stainless steel

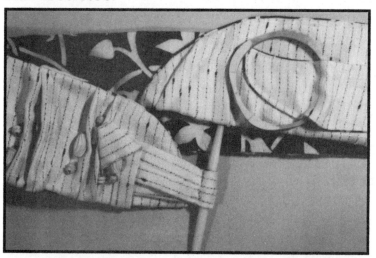

bone/brass bracelet with long bone bead

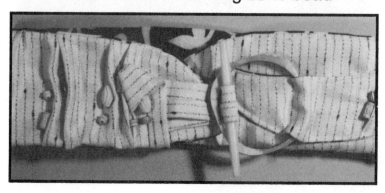

POSSIBILITIES:

Lacing

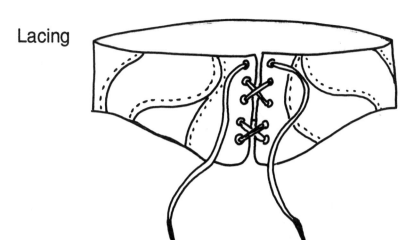

When lacing is to be the closure, eyelets or grommets can be used to reinforce the openings.

Another option would be large hooks or eyes. The laces would be looped around the hooks... or threaded thru the eyes.

Shoelaces or rolled leather are choices for lacing ... there is also cording in a variety of sizes.

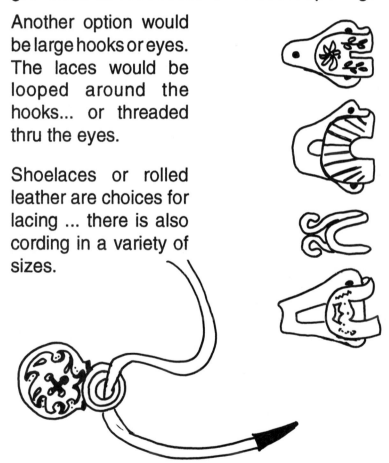

Pewter loops, as seen on costumes or sweaters, may be found in knitting, button or import shops. They look like a button with a loop on one side.

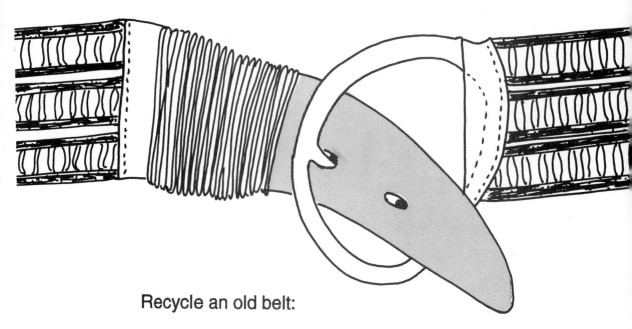

Recycle an old belt:

Combine elastic with the two ends of an old belt.

First measure the elastic (one wide piece or 3 or 4 rows of a narrower one) that will fit the vertical space of the two ends. Stretch elastic slightly to comfortably fit the waist.

Cut the old belt where desired. Keep in mind that the cut ends will have to be attached to the new part of the belt.

In this case, several elastic pieces are sewn to the leather ends.

If fabric is chosen, instead of elastic, then the belt wouldn't be expandable. Careful measurements would need to be taken so the belt would fit properly.

Combinations are unlimited for creating belts by recycling, for casual to very dressy.

It doesn't matter if sale or thrift store belts fit. Save the ends. The fastener is already there... just cut and add the elastic.

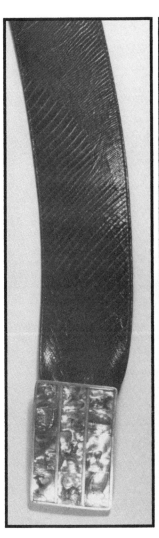 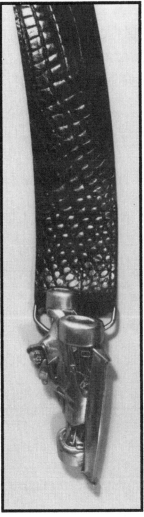 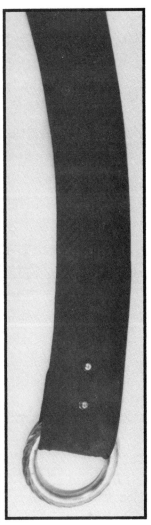

Leather belts can be updated and a new buckle can give it needed pizazz. Simply take off the old buckle, find a beautiful new one that is about the same size. Slip the end thru the buckle opening and fasten with leather glue.

The pearl and silver buckle is originally from Mexico. The brass racing car was a gift from a student from Australia. The third belt has a new look with a brass bracelet. The flat end just slides thru the bracelet, the stud-like protrusions fasten into the holes.

The black leather belt has a new brass buckle and two processed frog skins. The skins are folded in half. Holes are punched just beyond the belt width. Brass fasteners (from the office supply) are set into the holes and bent back. The bent ends are covered with a strip of soft leather so the back will be smooth. To wear the narrow belt plain, simply slide the frog skin 'tubes' off.

Lizard, or other leather pieces may be used as well.... or these overlapping pieces could be fabric collage or sections of woven strips. The idea is a good one, use it to suit yourself.

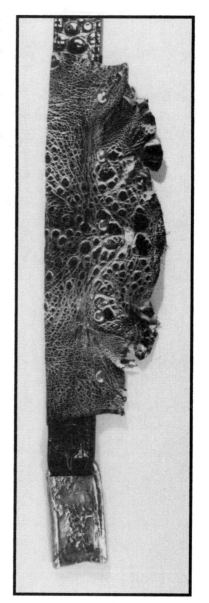

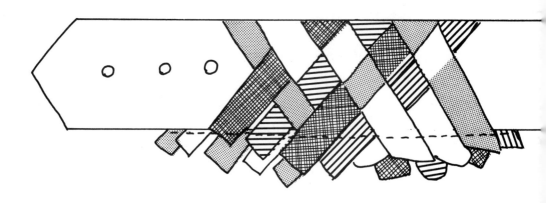

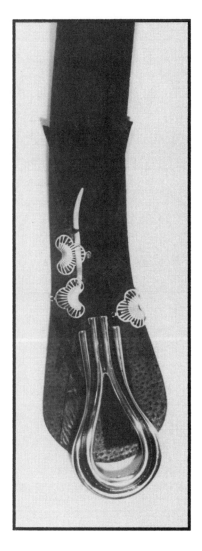

Black suede is dressed up with brass pieces and buckle. Textured leather strips are glued on as a contrast to the suede.

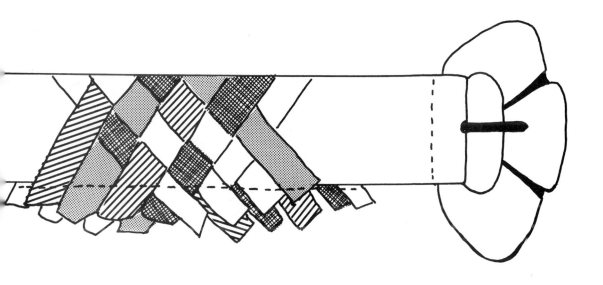

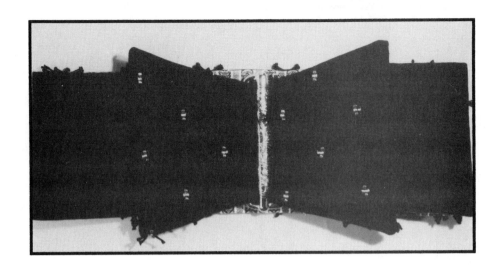

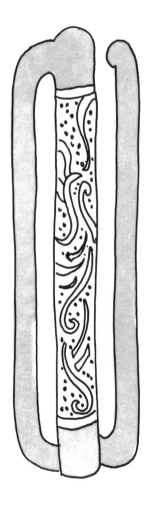

This belt is made of heavy cotton called appropriately 'bow-tie' since the shape is just that. The front sections fold back. The belt was made to fit the depth of the long buckle, the drawing is the actual size.

A tube-like opening on one side, slides onto the 'buckle' to fasten. Silver beads and satin stitching with metallic threads relate to the chrome fastener.

Black moire taffeta is a basic straight belt with a triangle shape at each end. A two-part buckle from the 40's was the start for the bow tie belt. A small pleat narrows the end to fit the buckle. Gold satin stitching and narrow braid embellish this dressy belt.

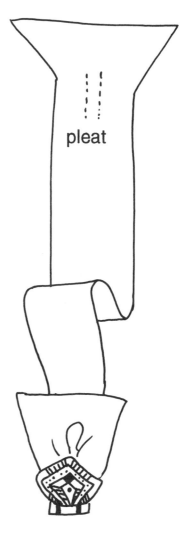

pleat

The triangle shaped ends fold back to form the bow tie.

Note: The same pattern is used for belt on the opposite page (without the pleat).

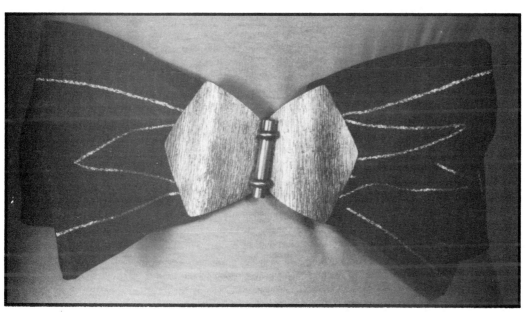

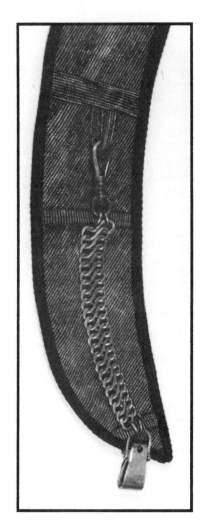

Stonewashed ribbed denim makes a great casual belt. This style fits below the waist. The edges are finished with bias in dark blue textured cotton. The fastener is a vintage chain with clips at each end. This was a second-hand store find. I don't know what it's design function <u>was</u>......... it's always a challenge to make it <u>be</u> something else.

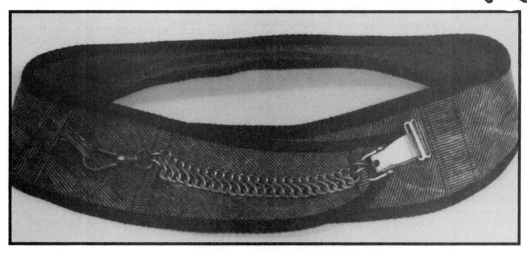

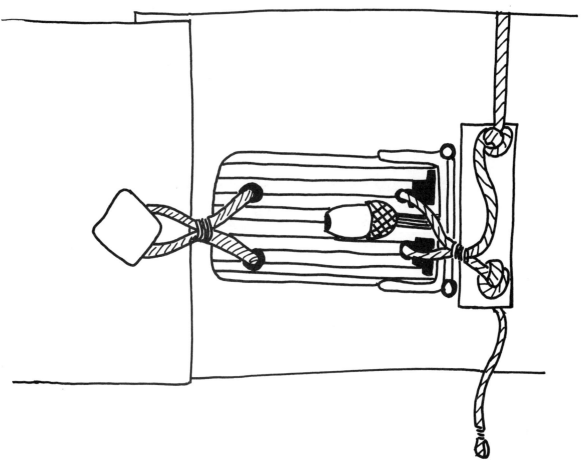

Finding a wonderful treasure that has closure potential is half the fun. The other half is, of course, figuring out how to use it. This brass piece had been an old album hinge. There were six holes in it so fastening to something would be easy. Covered cording seemed to be just the right choice to connect the metal piece to the fabric. The cording loops around and is wrapped and knotted, hand stitched to keep it in place. The loop on the left side is the 'buttonhole' that fastens to the square button.

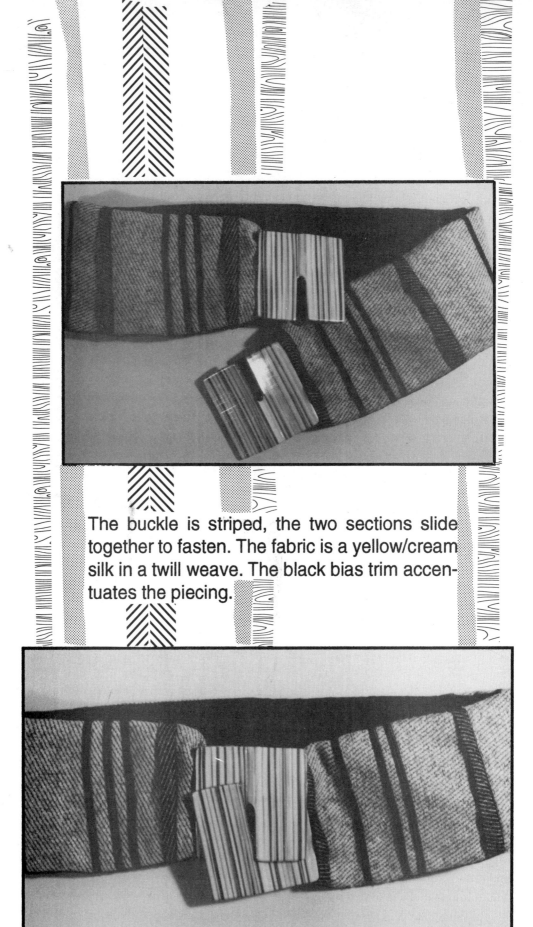

The buckle is striped, the two sections slide together to fasten. The fabric is a yellow/cream silk in a twill weave. The black bias trim accentuates the piecing.

Fancy elastics are a good choice for an easy, quick, one-size-fits-all belt. Cut the elastic slightly smaller than the waist size, make sure that it's comfortable before it is cut. Slide the ends of the elastic thru the buckle and stitch in place. Since the belt is rather plain the copper buckle sets it off nicely.

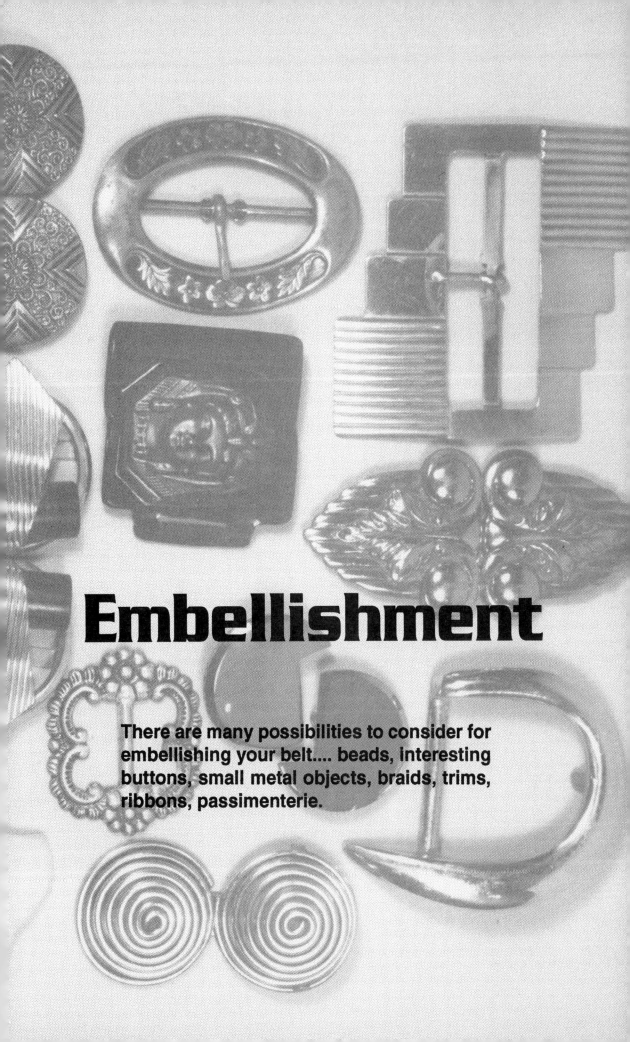

Embellishment

There are many possibilities to consider for embellishing your belt.... beads, interesting buttons, small metal objects, braids, trims, ribbons, passimenterie.

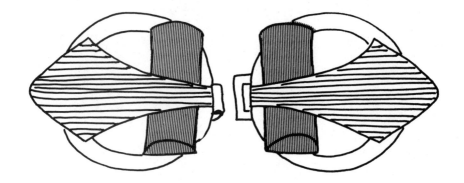

The design on the button or object could be the design inspiration for the belt. When adding beads, buttons or other objects remember to choose wisely, do the objects relate to the general 'feeling' of the belt? Make the object or embellishment an integral part of the belt.

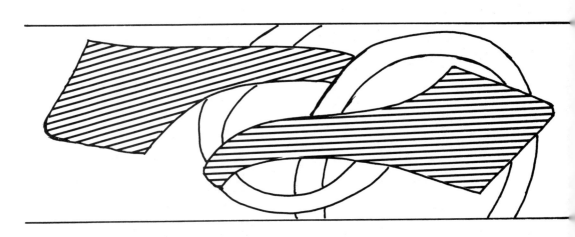

Having a large collection of antique buckles and buttons, as well as unusual metal, wood, bone pieces, is a definite advantage. These can be the focal point of the belt, the items that make the belts unique. Where to find them? Antique stores, second-hand stores, flea markets, garage sales to name but a few.....look in stores that sell hardware, sporting goods, boating supplies.

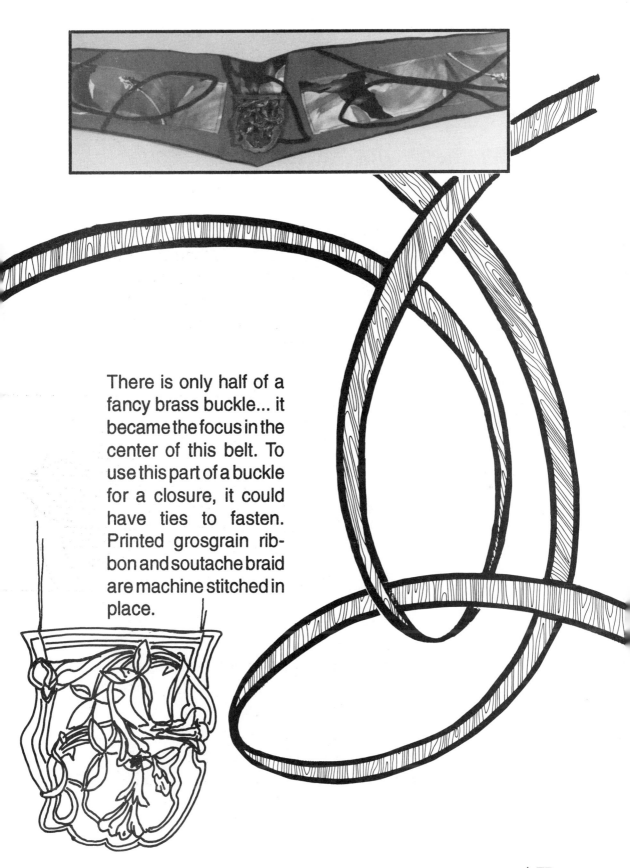

There is only half of a fancy brass buckle... it became the focus in the center of this belt. To use this part of a buckle for a closure, it could have ties to fasten. Printed grosgrain ribbon and soutache braid are machine stitched in place.

This narrow belt is made of oriental brocade in bright colors, with commercial belting inside. The embellishment is a gold watch fob and chain plus enamelled green beads. Assorted brass pieces also dangle from the side of the belt. The fastener is a gold colored metal buckle.

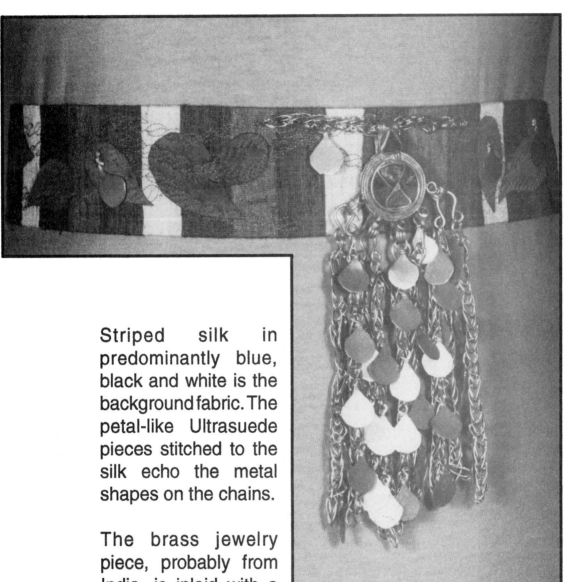

Striped silk in predominantly blue, black and white is the background fabric. The petal-like Ultrasuede pieces stitched to the silk echo the metal shapes on the chains.

The brass jewelry piece, probably from India, is inlaid with a lapis mosaic. The design of the unusual chain is repeated with the machine stitching pattern.

This handcarved wooden container was designed to be attached to a belt. There are many items that could be used like this in a utilitarian way or merely a decorative one.

In the 1800's, chatelaines were popular. This was a hook-like clasp with a chain that fastened to a belt to hold keys, scissors, and other implements used in the household. Some were very elegantly made of sterling silver, others were more ordinary and made of pewter or other metals. Often the housekeeper had a chatelaine to keep her 'tools' within easy reach.

Small purses on special clips were also used on belts to carry change and other items. To enlarge on that idea we now have 'fanny packs' and other similar carry-alls.

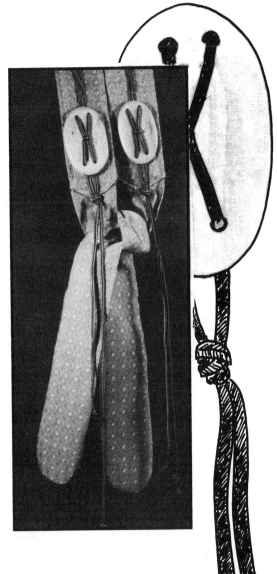

Silk necktie fabric is the background material for this straight belt with ties. The smooth rosewood ovals were drilled to accomodate the soutache braid that is threaded through. Beads embellish the junctions of the soutache braid. The long braid and the silk ties can both be tied or the soutache can be left to hang free.

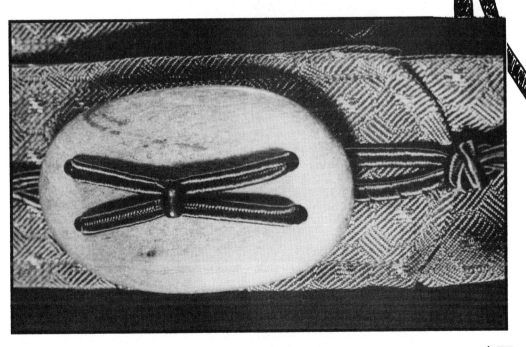

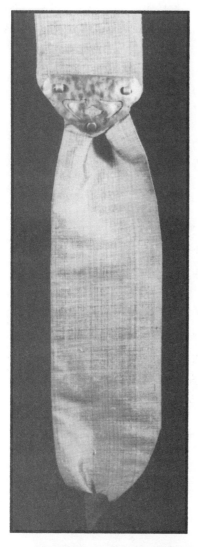

This belt is made with handwoven silk fabric with some metallic threads to make the pattern. The front ends are shaped like the dull brass pieces attached at the front edge. The flattened cone shapes at the tie ends are also brass.

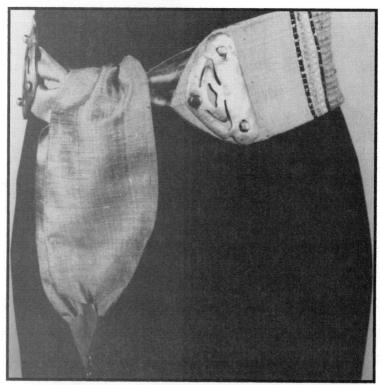

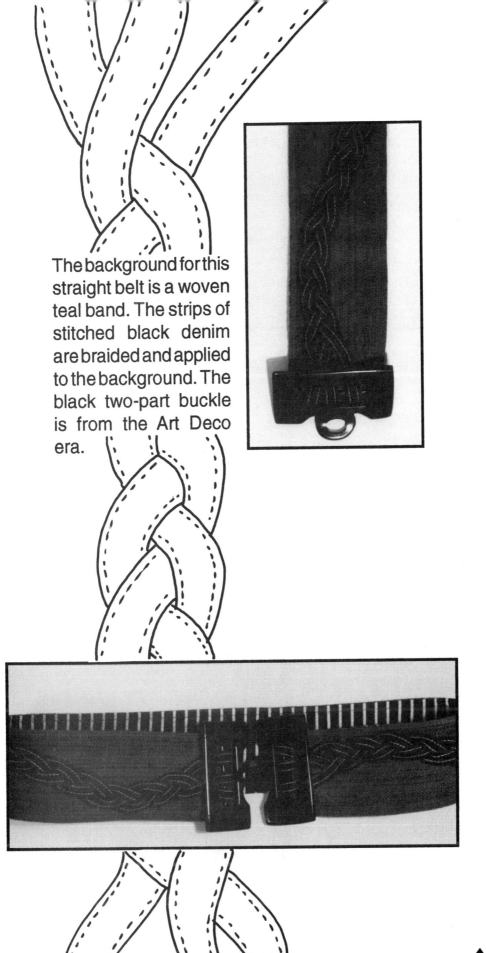

The background for this straight belt is a woven teal band. The strips of stitched black denim are braided and applied to the background. The black two-part buckle is from the Art Deco era.

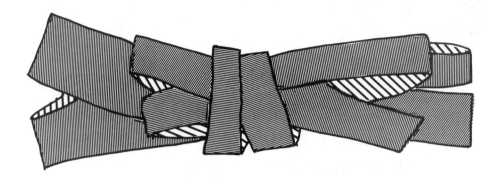

This narrow rhinestone belt was too small for the owner so it was passed on to me. Obviously this short belt needed to be made longer and more interesting. I made a straight plain belt of black velveteen. The rhinestone belt was hand stitched in place. Three long rectangles are lined with grey and silver striped taffeta and folded to apply as a 'bow'. The buckle adds dimension.

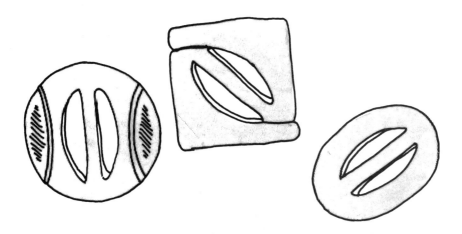

The problem: what to do with dozens of small pearl buckles?

A solution: thread them onto some horsehair braid and handsew them to the cotton fabric.

The horsehair braid is very flexible so it works well on the rounded lines of the fabric and also relates to the round shapes of the buckles. The braid is usually not used as a decorative element, that's what makes it interesting.

Horsehair braid is sold by the yard or in packages in yardage stores. It is available in black or white.

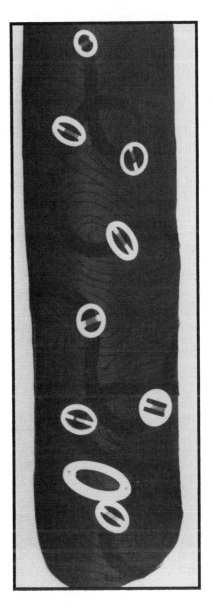

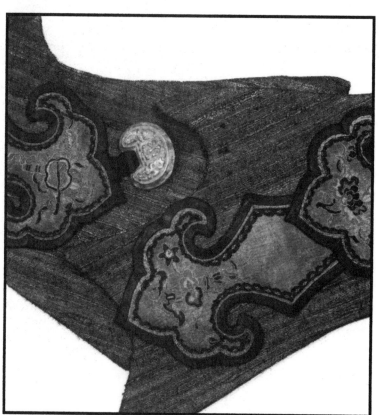

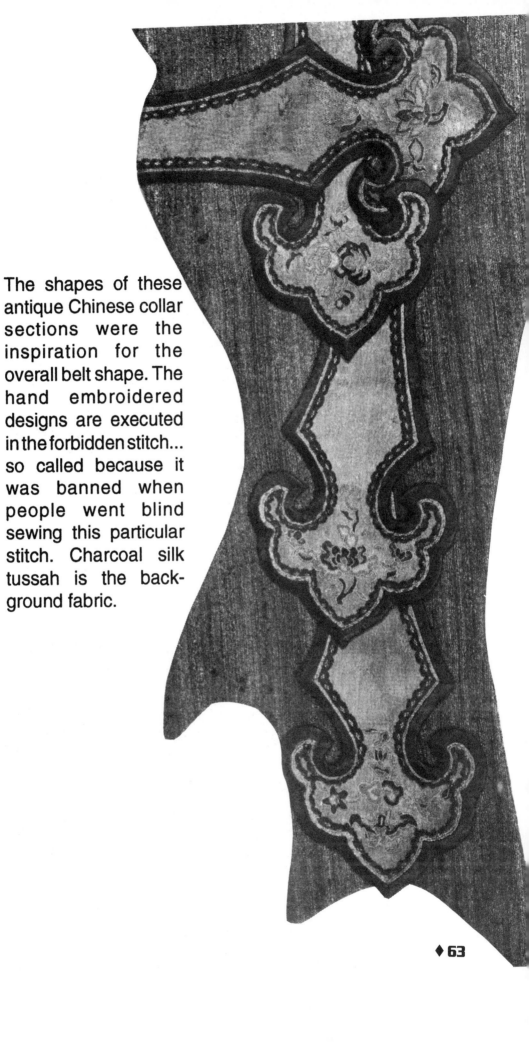

The shapes of these antique Chinese collar sections were the inspiration for the overall belt shape. The hand embroidered designs are executed in the forbidden stitch... so called because it was banned when people went blind sewing this particular stitch. Charcoal silk tussah is the background fabric.

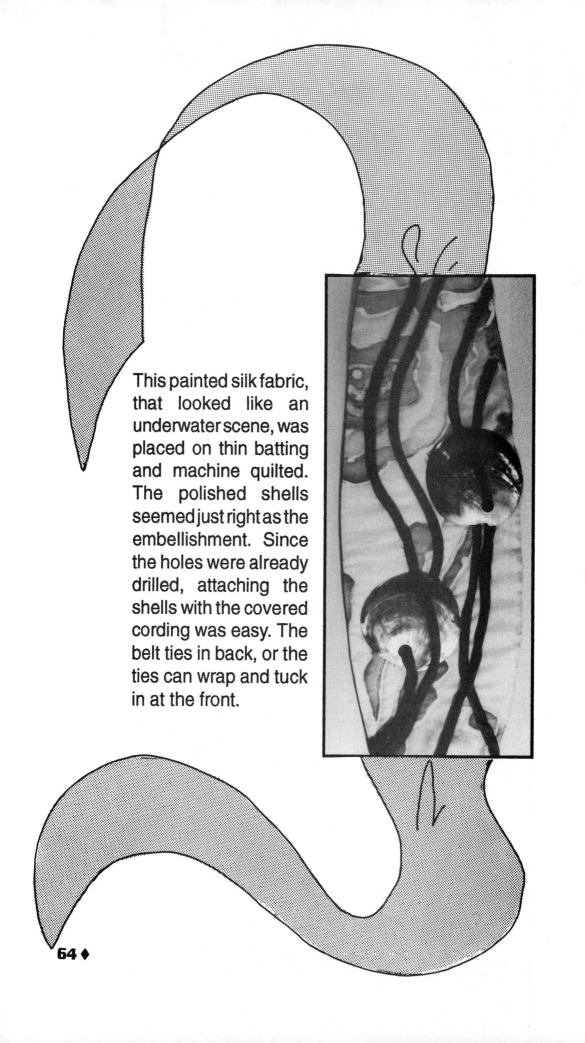

This painted silk fabric, that looked like an underwater scene, was placed on thin batting and machine quilted. The polished shells seemed just right as the embellishment. Since the holes were already drilled, attaching the shells with the covered cording was easy. The belt ties in back, or the ties can wrap and tuck in at the front.

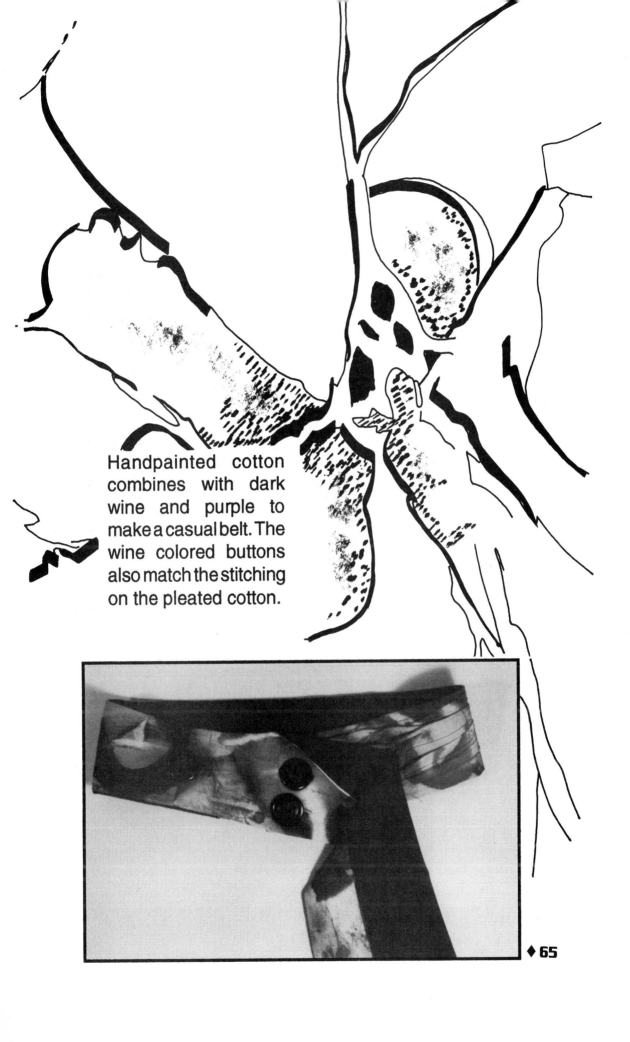

Handpainted cotton combines with dark wine and purple to make a casual belt. The wine colored buttons also match the stitching on the pleated cotton.

The cats are a rubber stamp that have been 'colored in' using permanent markers. What an easy technique! The buckle is from the 30's and commercial belting is the interfacing.

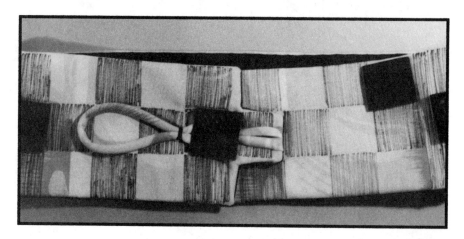

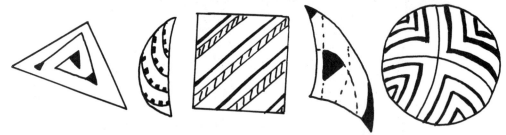

For this belt, a stencil was cut from a stiff plastic sheet. The squares are placed where desired and the space is filled in with the colored pens, as the cats. The purpose of the stencil is to keep the image sharp, to help you 'stay inside the lines'. Try various designs on different fabrics... such as a subtle print, as above or muted stripes in addition to plain fabrics. Match buttons with the shape and/or the design of the button for the colored lines that you add.

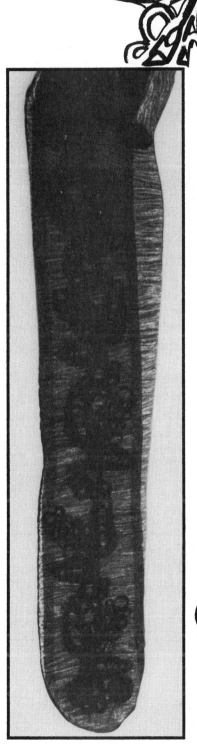

Purple and gold metallic fabric is mushroom pleated to create a wonderful texture. Fragile black antique passimenterie pieces are covered with black silk organza for protection. A few beads are sewn in place to add a little sparkle.

Techniques

The following information is presented to pique your interest, nudge your creativity and expand your basic sewing skills. Your interpretation of this data and your design ability will combine to create fabulous fashion accessories.

stitching

Topstitching is a very easy technique to use for professional results. Repetitive lines of stitching in a pattern is an excellent method to easily change the surface of your fabric and enhance your design.

♦ 71

STITCHING:

Machine stitching is an easy, fast way to add color, texture & design to your belt project.

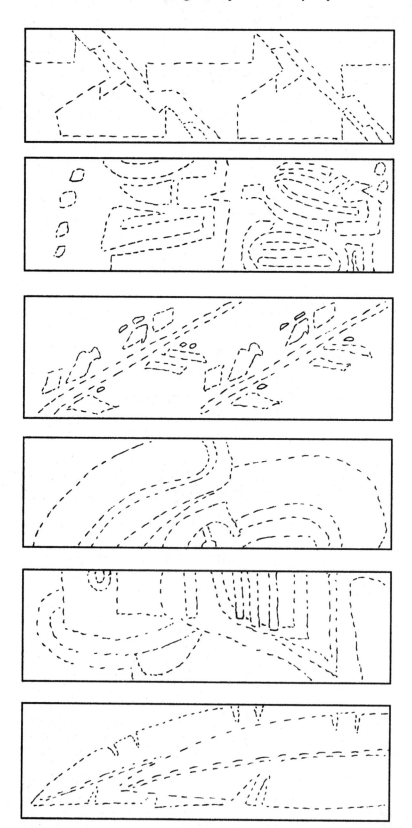

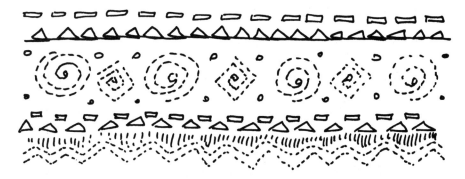

Free-motion machine embroidery is easier than I thought it would be and not as time consuming as I anticipated. Draw a few lines with a 'disappearing' pen as the starting point for the design. For a quilted effect, use Thermore or other light batting under the fashion fabric.

Lower the feed dog and put on the darning foot. If you don't have one or don't use any foot at all, lower the presser foot anyway. Use a hoop if desired. If the fabric and underlining are quite firm, the hoop may be unnecessary and the fabric will be easier to move around as you sew.

Sew on the lines you have drawn as the pattern. Fill in the spaces of the design with more stitching. Accentuating the shapes will make them stand out, especially if there is batting or flannel underneath. Clear or 'invisible' thread may be used if the design warrants it.

Cording or other fancy threads and yarns can be added to the fashion fabric after the main design has been sewn. Patterned sewing machine stitches can be used effectively with this free-motion stitching. The rigid machine patterns can have a more fluid look when combined with free-motion stitching.

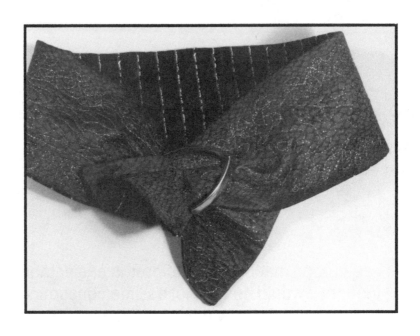

The drapery weight cotton/rayon fabric was printed with a lizard-like design. Gold all over free-motion stitching was added to coordinate with the wishbone shaped buckle. The belt is lined with black/red striped cotton.

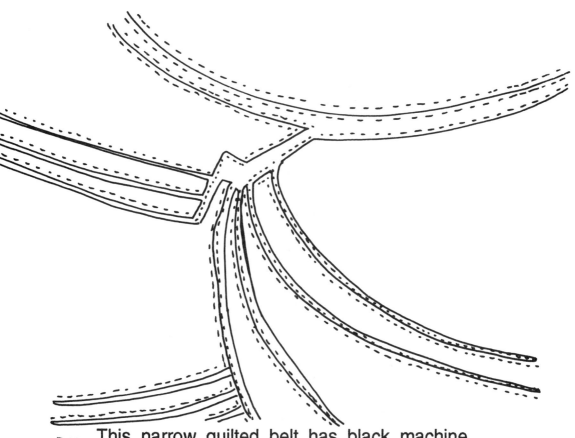

This narrow quilted belt has black machine stitching around the printed designs. The Japanese cotton is enhanced with the brass beads and the 30's buckle.

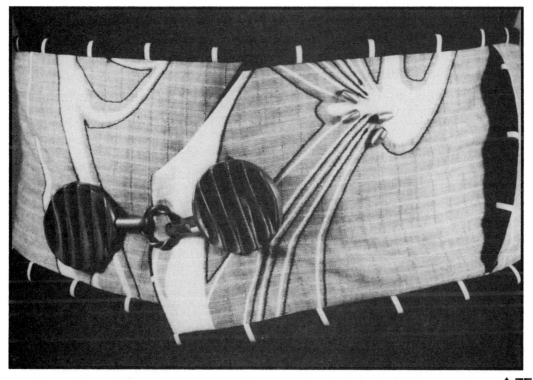

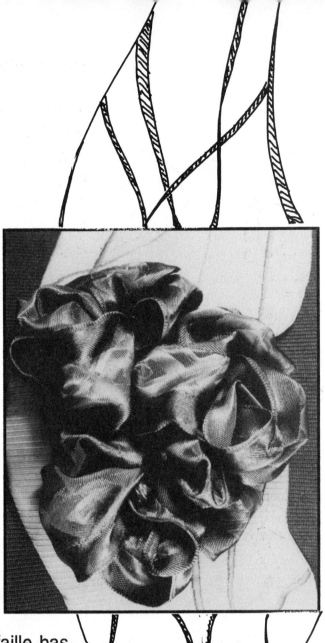

The red silk faille has purple satin stitching to match the lining. The flower shapes are made of French ribbon. The ribbon has wire edges so the flowers can be revitalized by rounding out the petals.

Ribbon Flower

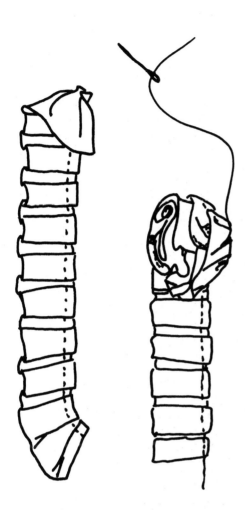

1. Start with 1/3 to 1/2 yd. of ribbon. The first example shown uses box pleated ribbon, but any ribbon will work if it is gathered on one edge.

The second example shows bias cut fabric about 12" long, (use something crisp, i.e. organza or netting) that is folded lengthwise and gathered on the curved edge.

2. Begin by folding the raw edge down to catch with needle and thread. Now roll the ribbon or fabric tightly around itself, fastening with several stitches at each turn of the ribbon.

3. Continue rolling and sewing, keeping the ribbon or fabric loose to make the outer edges flare out. The 'petals' can be folded, if desired.

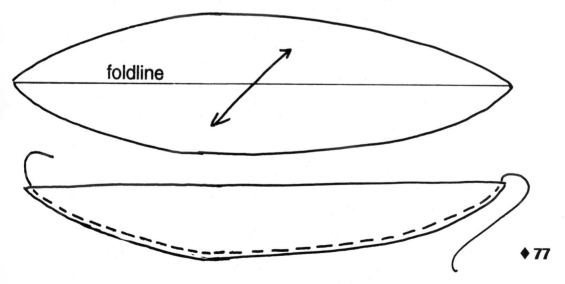

foldline

tucks

Tucks can be used to change a fabric surface remarkably, especially if the fabric is a bold stripe. The stripes make it easy ... just fold, stitch, and press to create a very optical look.

Plain or subtle prints can be tucked and stitched to add interest to an otherwise ordinary fabric. Make the next sewing project an eyecatching one by adding tucks to the techniques to be included. Stitch the tucks with some of the decorative stitches that are available on your machine, or use satin stitches in various widths. Add ribbon or other small inserts as the tucks are sewn in to create a design.

Varying the sizes of the tucks and the width of the stitching will give the fabric surface a more artistic look.

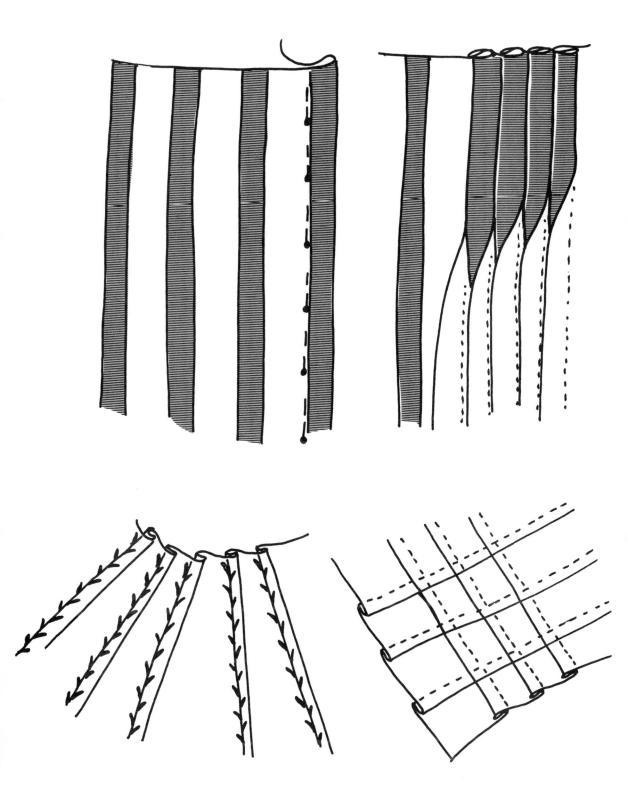

These tucked pieces were the scraps 'left-over' from another project. The pieces weren't cut out -- simply faced and arranged to make a belt-like shape. Then the pieces were sewn together.

The closure is a flat horn bracelet with ties to fasten.

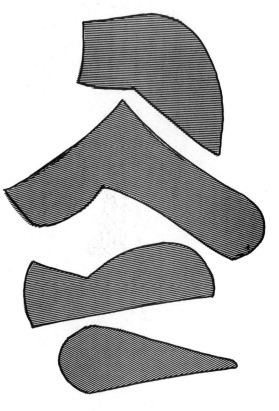

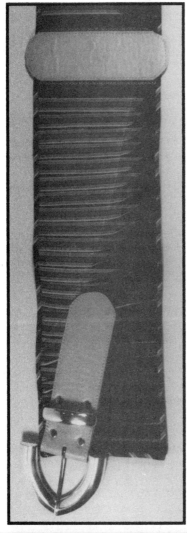

Tucks are sewn in the striped cotton fabric to exaggerate the contrast in the colors. The edges are finished with a bias strip of the striped fabric. The ends of a recycled leather belt were cut off and sewn in place to fasten. A small piece of leather, also cut from the 'old' belt, is applied in the center.

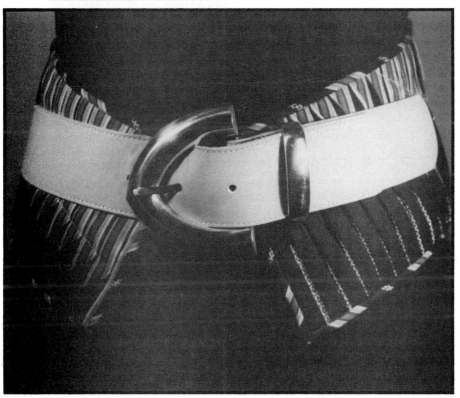

pleats

Pleats are basically made by creasing and folding a fabric. Pin and press the pleats in place. Measuring each pleat is rather tedious, but necessary if you wish to have uniform sizes. If you have a cloth pleater, simply place the fabric wrong side up... pleat where desired and press on some iron-on interfacing to keep the pleats in place.

Pleats may then be stitched in a pattern....
        may be held in place with faced shapes
        may be embellished with braids/trims
        may be manipulated to create texture.

One of the many possibilities with the pleating technique would be to change the fabric some- how before pleating....by gathering, by folding, by piecing or ?

Pleats are made in this brocade fabric. Fan shapes are cut to coincide with the metal pieces. Silk organza is placed over the entire belt and the lining is applied. The metal shapes are sewn in place. The two-part buckle looks pleated also.... how's that for relationships?

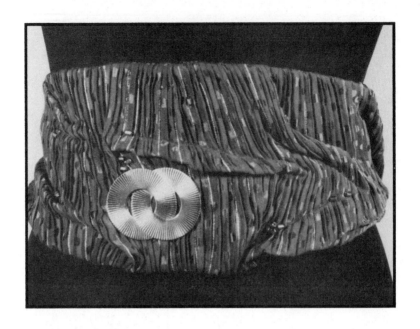

This fabric is permanently pleated in a mushroom style pleat by a commercial establishment. To change the texture slightly, tunnels have been stitched and a few beads are sewn on. The pleated looking pin was added as the embellishment.

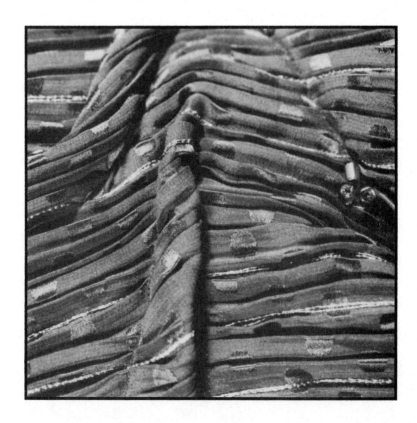

The gray/green silk fabric is gathered in a swirled random configuration. Then it's pleated, with the cloth pleater, and stitched. Silver beads, narrow cord and silver metallic thread embellish the belt.

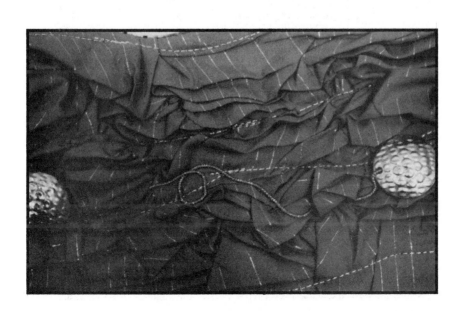

tunnels

Tunnels is what I call this technique because it looks like a tunnel of fabric. The concept is that a layer of fashion fabric is placed on top of an underlining or interfacing in the case of a belt. The two layers are stitched together at one side. The top layer is picked up and moved to create a tunnel of fabric. Pin the tunnel in place and stitch.

The tunnels can be close together or there can be flat spaces between leaving space for multiple rows of stitching. These tunnels can be stuffed with batting or cording. Various trims, braids and beads could embellish the tunnels, in addition to the stitching.

Consider piecing the fabric before tunnelling or cutting up the tunnelled fabric to make a pieced belt with added texture.

This straight belt is made of cream colored silk suiting with a black slub. Tunnels accentuate the black lines. The bone beads relate to the bracelet and a long bead that make the closure. The closure pieces are held in place with faced shapes.

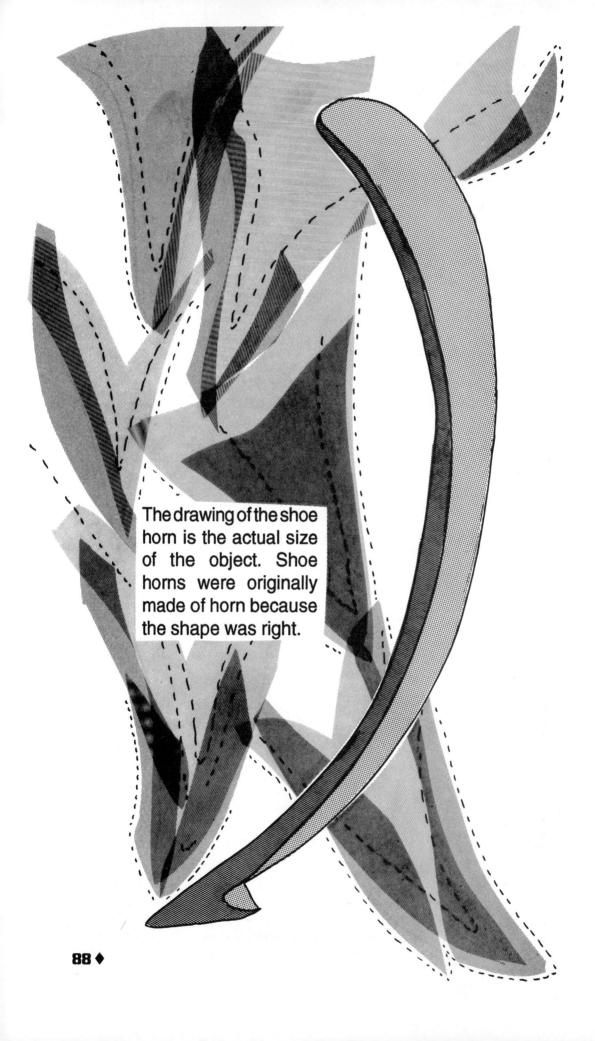

The drawing of the shoe horn is the actual size of the object. Shoe horns were originally made of horn because the shape was right.

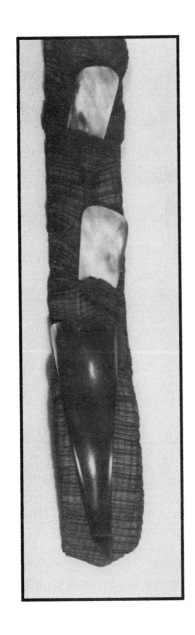

This shoe horn was cut and drilled to fasten it to the belt. The fabric is sheer wool that has elastic thread in it to make the tiny pleats. Tunneling is the technique used to create the texture of the wool.

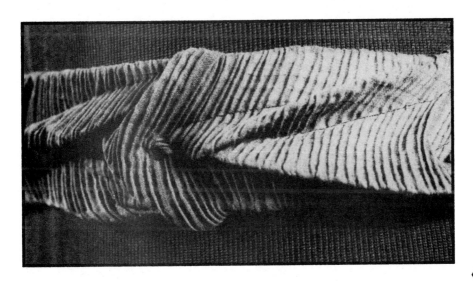

wrinkled/stitched

This particular technique works best on natural fibers because they wrinkle easily and stay wrinkled. Since we will only be concerned with using small pieces, I will show you a quick method. Twist, pleat, or crumple a scrap of fabric that is to be a part of a belt. Pin it to the ironing board and press firmly. Let it cool.

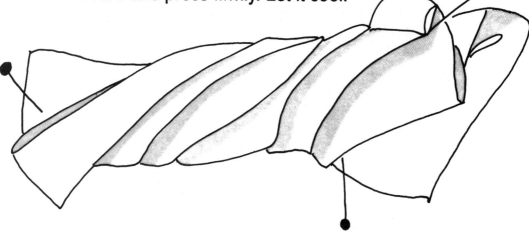

On the cut-out belt interfacing, place a few pieces of fusible material (i.e. Wonder-Under). Arrange the wrinkled scraps of fabric on top and press onto the fusible. Stitch as desired.

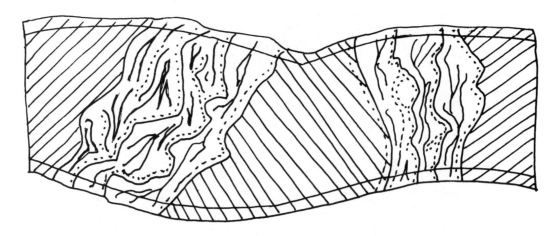

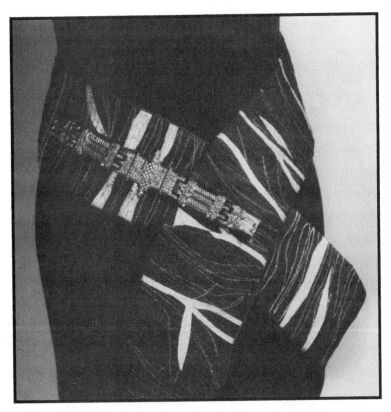

Black taffeta is wrinkled and stitched with copper colored thread to a firm backing material. Narrow cut shapes of copper fabric are applied. The fabulous two part copper buckle is attached to this shaped belt that is worn below the waist.

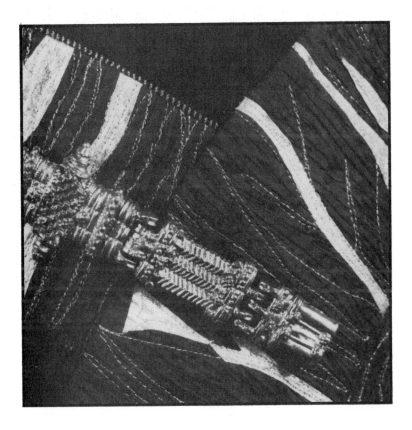

faced shapes

One of the techniques that I use more than any other is one that I call faced shapes. It is a method of finishing the edges and defining them with a contrasting color or fabric. The facings may be bias strips if the shapes are simple ones. I usually use stripes for the bias facings, for the graphic appeal.

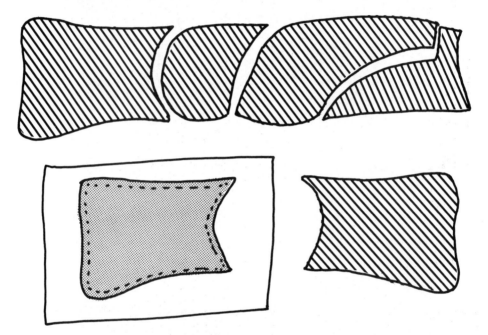

If the whole piece is to be faced all around, stitch and trim. Cut a small hole in the middle of the back of the facing and pull thru. Press and stitch in the appropriate place. If only one or two sides is to be faced, stitch and trim ... turn thru one of the remaining openings.

This is the perfect method to use when adding pieces that need to be finished on a belt. A bit of color to add some pizazz... or an edge to be finished in a flash.

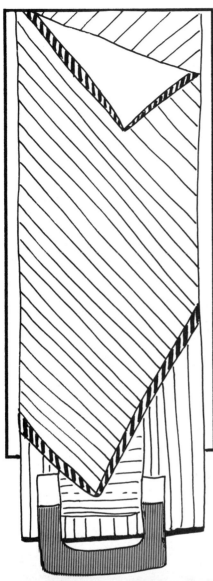

Black and white cotton bias strips finish and define the edges of this black ribbed cotton belt. The large enamelled buckle, with a prong underneath, hooks in eyelets to fasten.

A beautiful Chinese brocade, in predominate shades of red, is the start of this belt. Purple satin stitching is added to the designs on the silk fabric to relate to the textured purple fabric to be used on the belt. Some of the circles are cut out and faced to overlay the shapes. The textured weave in purple and black are the cone shapes at the ends of the belt. The lining curves over the top of the belt to look almost collar-like. The fastener is an antique Chinese buckle — an exquisite 'find'.

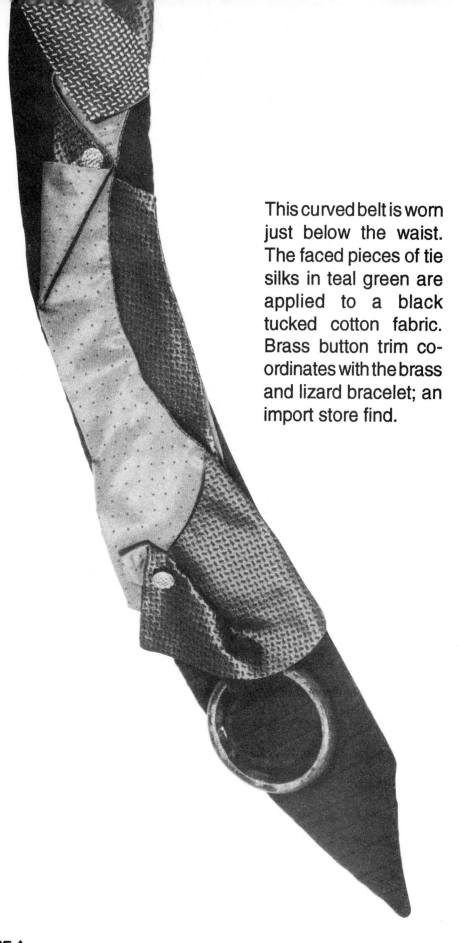

This curved belt is worn just below the waist. The faced pieces of tie silks in teal green are applied to a black tucked cotton fabric. Brass button trim coordinates with the brass and lizard bracelet; an import store find.

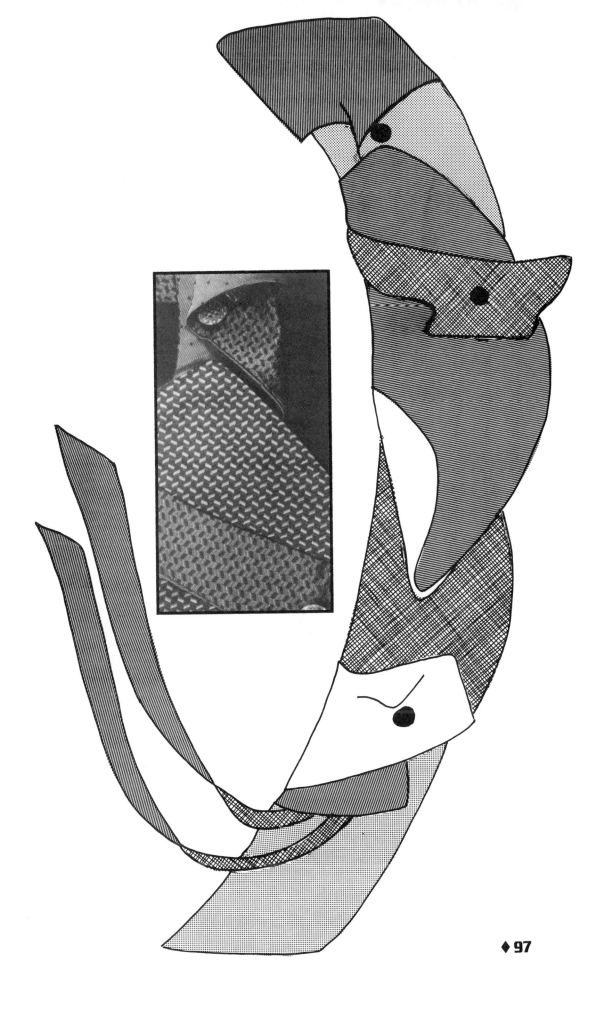

Beaded passimenterie pieces from a 30's belt are updated. They are sewn to grey/green silk faille shapes that echo the beaded medallions. Small brass buttons add the finishing touch where the shapes overlap. The belt shapes are lined with black and gray chintz.

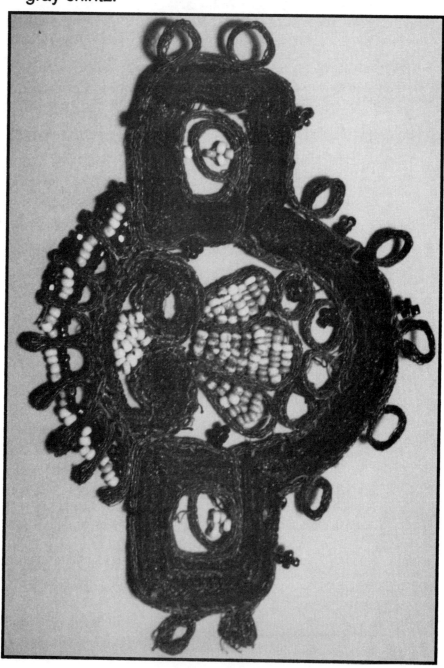

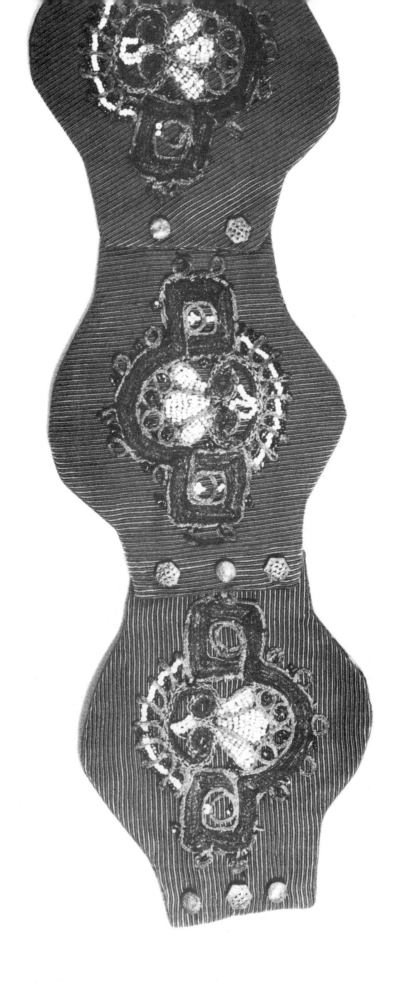

piecing

Piecing or patchwork is one method for putting sections of fabric together as in a collage. When using this technique, it is easiest to start at one end of the belt ... stitching and overlapping the shapes directly on the interfacing. If the closure is to be included in one of the overlapping shapes, plan accordingly and include the ties or other fasteners when it's appropriate.

Small cut pieces can be overlapped with no thought of finishing the edges. The ravelled edges would be showing and the added texture could be a great addition to the belt.

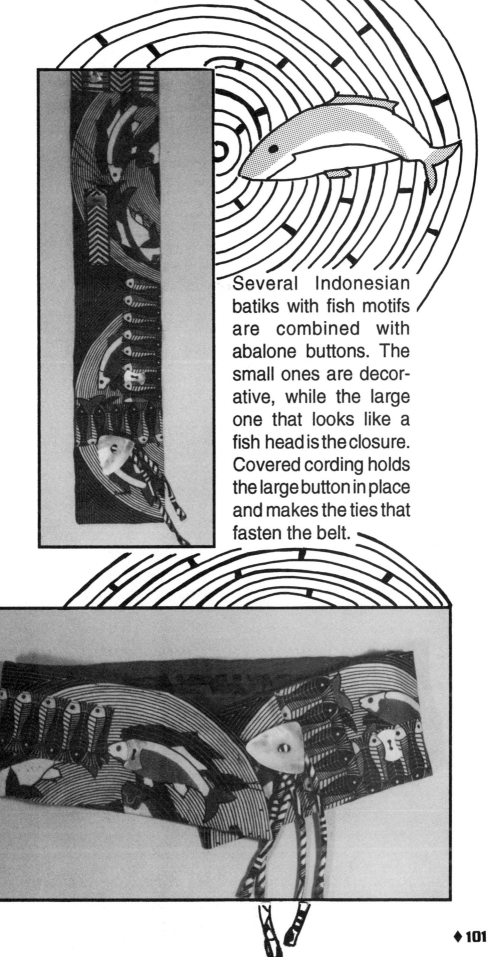

Several Indonesian batiks with fish motifs are combined with abalone buttons. The small ones are decorative, while the large one that looks like a fish head is the closure. Covered cording holds the large button in place and makes the ties that fasten the belt.

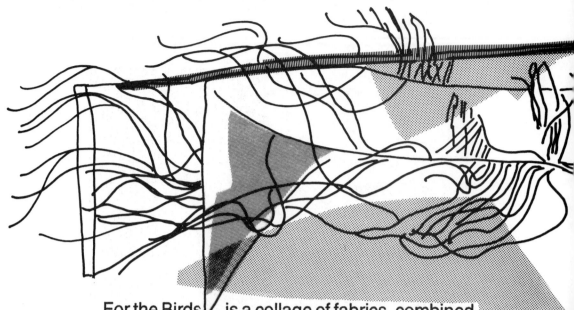

For the Birds!... is a collage of fabrics, combined with some sheer overlay. The fringe is the back side of a brocade obi from Japan. The long floats of thread are cut to create the fringe. A button that looks exactly like an eye (what a find) and a few beads finish this belt.

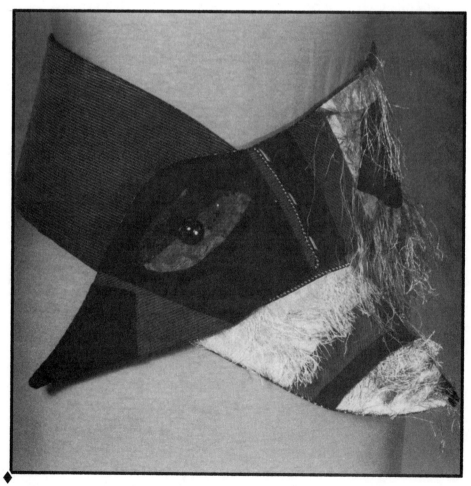

Cotton stripes are combined and stitched to enhance the stripes. The focal point of this belt is an old drawer pull from an antique store. The metal piece is sewn in place with large black beads. The long tabs of fabric opposite, tie onto the handle of the drawer pull.

The stripes in the black and white cotton denim are arranged to create movement. The red leather at each end takes advantage of the irregular shapes. Slits are cut to allow the ties to come thru. Striped glass buttons are sewn on -- nice relationship. The belt is lined with an abstract horse print.

Black and white 1" stripes are made into checks. To make the checks, cut the fabric in strips across the stripes. The size of the checks is the size of the width of the stripes, in this case 1". Add seam allowances. Align by alternating the two colors, pin and sew.

The other fabrics in the belt are pieced and stitched lengthwise. A brass swivel clip is the closure, it fastens to several brass rings.The rings are held in place with a black braid that is also the ornament on the back of the belt. When it is worn the top third folds down to look like a collar.

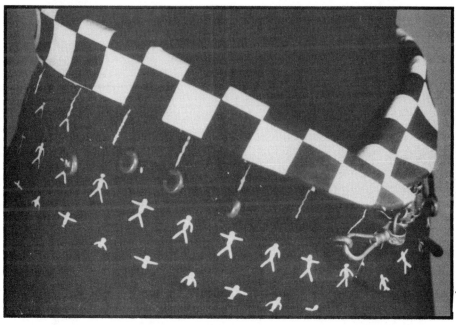

tubes/strips

Tubes and strips of fabric can be used effectively to create a texture. These tubes or strips can be woven, applied to cover the unfinished edges of cut shapes or to emphasize the design on your belt.

To make the tubes, cut the fabric about 2 1/2" to 3" wide. In the case of stripes I cut the fabric lengthwise, crosswise or on the bias to gain the effect that I want. Fold the tubes in half lengthwise and stitch. Turn and press. Pin the tubes in place, close together at one end of the belt or in the section designated to be woven. Weave across, over and under, pinning the tubes at each end.

Torn strips of fabric can also be used effectively. Simply tear the fabric into strips of the desired width and weave them. Topstitching can be used to minimize the amount of ravelling and to add interest.

Bias tubes or strips can be added for interest and design value. Apply by machine or hand stitching to the belt. These strips can be used to cover the unfinished edges of fabric shapes.

The tubes or strips can be combined with an object to create the closure that will integrate the fastener to the belt.

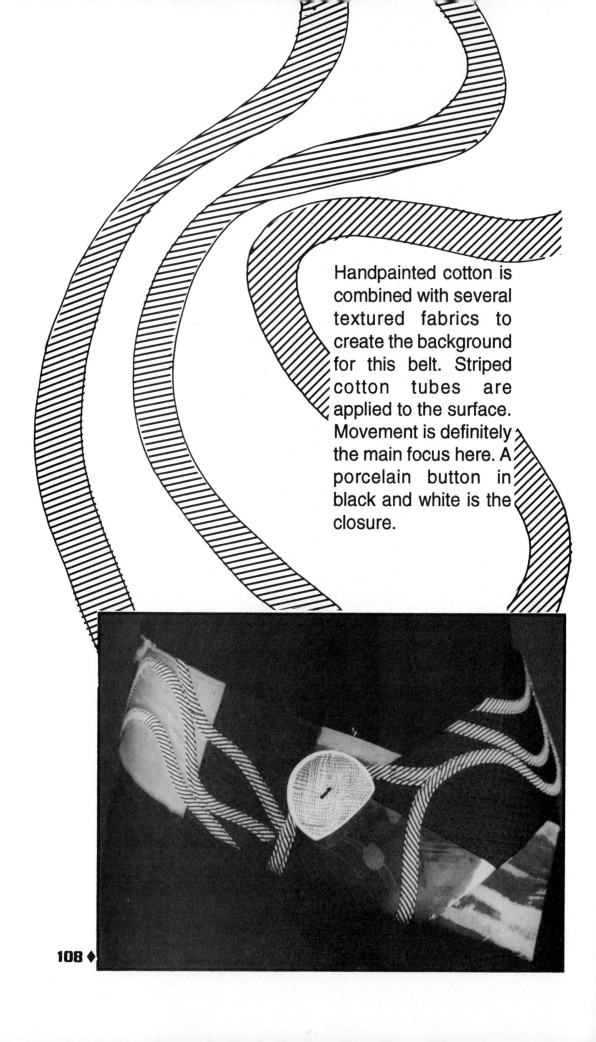

Handpainted cotton is combined with several textured fabrics to create the background for this belt. Striped cotton tubes are applied to the surface. Movement is definitely the main focus here. A porcelain button in black and white is the closure.

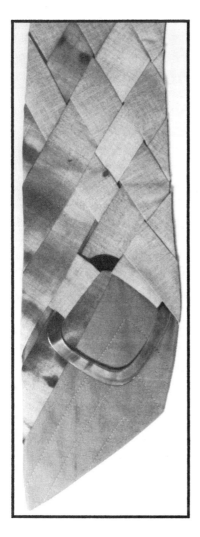

Handpainted cotton fabric is cut into strips then sewn as tubes and pressed. The tubes are woven together and applied to a backing, of the same fabric. The fastener is a flat horn bracelet that connects with the ties on the opposite side of the belt.

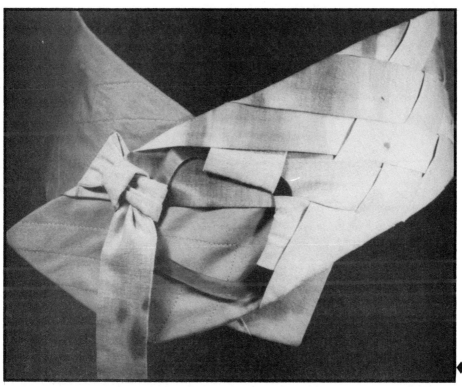

Three cotton fabrics are torn into strips, then woven. The strips are placed on an under-lining. To keep the raw edges from ravelling, the strips are machine stitched. Bias tubes emphasize the diagonal stitching lines. The ties are covered cording with large amber beads at the ends.

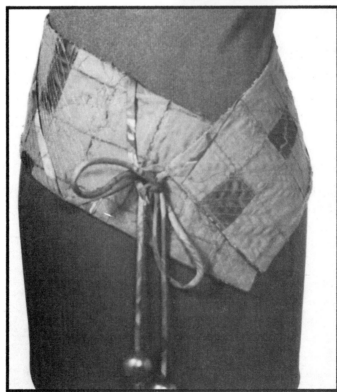

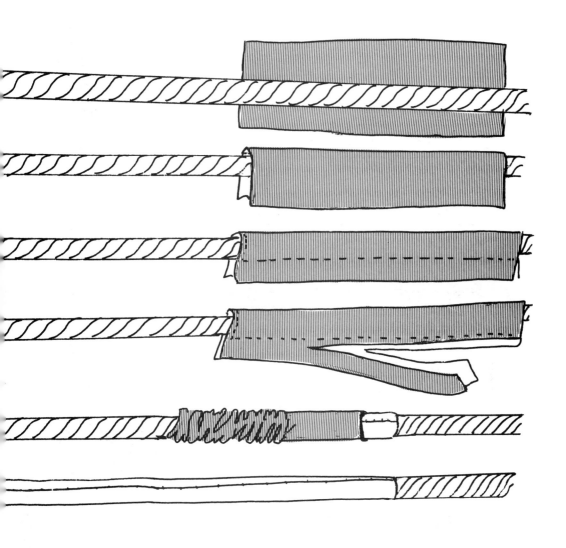

Tubes and strips may be used to make covered cording for ties and trims on a belt. To make the cording, cut bias strips four times the width of the cord. Measure from the end of the cord, the amount of bias to cover, then start with the second measure of cord. The bias will be stitched and turned to cover this first measure of cord. Fold the right side of the fabric over the cord. Using a zipper foot, stitch across the end and down the long side of the bias. When the fabric is a little heavy or hard to turn, it is helpful to stitch a rounded shape at the end of the short side as you turn the corner to the long side. Trim, being careful not to cut the cording. Slide fabric on cording and turn to the right side.

sheers

Sheer Joy! What fun to be able to use a luxurious fabric in a new way. Sheers are usually thought of when a special occasion arises like a wedding or a formal. I like to use the sheers, i.e. organza or chiffon, to change the colors of the fabric underneath or to protect a fragile antique piece.

My favorite application is to cover a collage of cut pieces and ravelled threads. There is no need to finish these in any way. Simply arrange the pieces in the design of your choice. There are two ways of keeping the collaged pieces in place.
1. Stitch the pieces randomly in place then cover with the sheer fabric.
2. Place collaged pieces on the backing. Cover with sheer fabric. Stitch thru all layers.

There is also an air of mystery about the garments... we're not always sure about what we are looking at... what is on top of what? I like that.

Each rectangle is a different collage design in silk. Stripes, plain and painted fabrics are combined. Each collage is covered with a silk organza overlay.

The metal pieces are sections of a necklace fastened with Chinese coins and brass fasteners. The sections are sewn together and the belt is lined. The tab at the end echoes the shape of the necklace pieces.

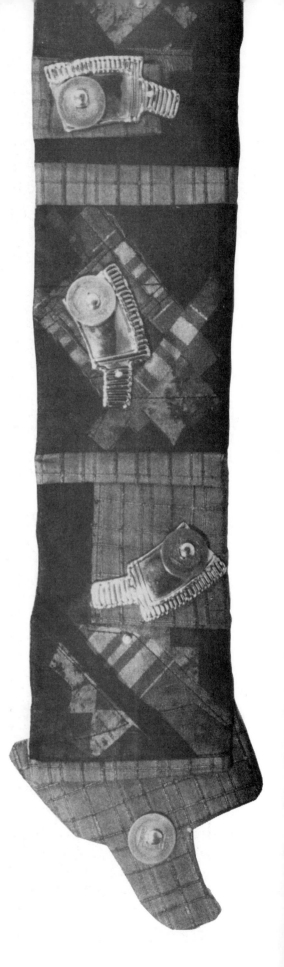

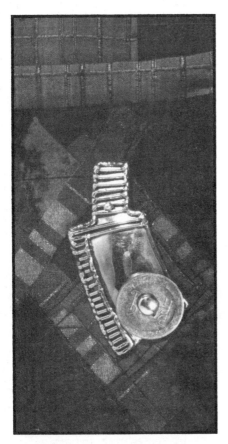

Several fabrics are layered to make this peplum style belt. On the firm foundation is a shiny green fabric, then a sheer with a leaf print.

Another sheer has black leaves woven in the sheer green organza. These leaves have been layered with a black organza with Wonder-Under sandwiched in between. The outer edges of the leaves are satin stitched together and cut out. These leaves are stitched in the center to create dimension. Several black braids are sewn on to simulate branches. Antique jet buttons with a flower design are the final touch (inset).

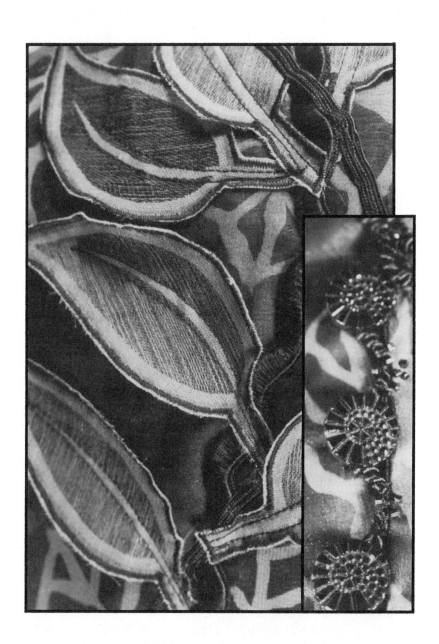

A graphic Japanese print is layered with a printed chiffon. The fabric loops, that are embellished with long brass beads, accomodate the narrow woven belt. This narrow belt ties and holds the overlapping wide belt in place.

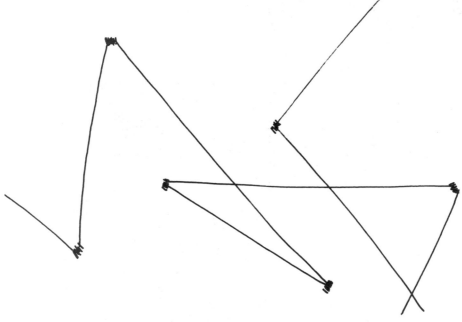

Black metallic printed satin and sheers were fused, with Wonder-Under then cut into rectangles and squares. These pieces are collaged to a firm foundation. Gold metallic threads are machine stitched using satin stitching and long floats of thread between. This holds all the layers together. A sheer fabric covers all. This ensures that the long floats will not be pulled or torn. Use a similar stitching design on top and cut the long floats. These will look like sparse fringe and will relate to the pattern underneath the sheer. The closure is a gold colored metal buckle.

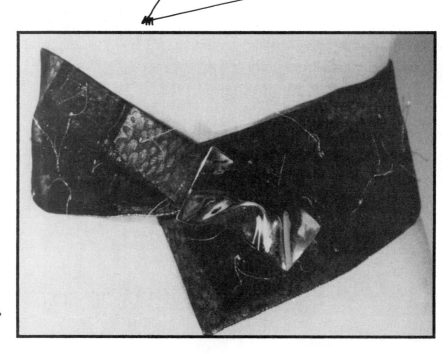

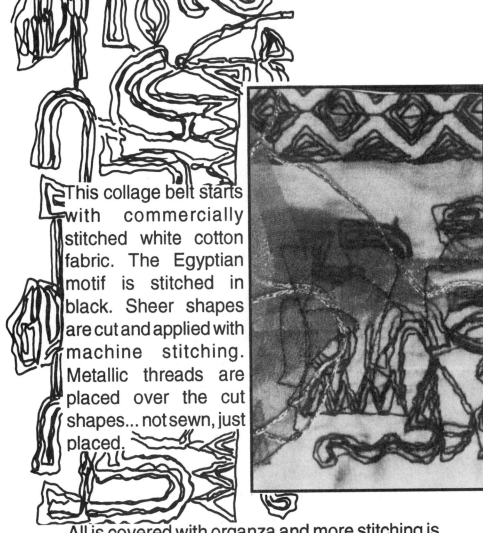

This collage belt starts with commercially stitched white cotton fabric. The Egyptian motif is stitched in black. Sheer shapes are cut and applied with machine stitching. Metallic threads are placed over the cut shapes... not sewn, just placed.

All is covered with organza and more stitching is added to keep all the layers together. The closure is a pearl and horn bracelet.

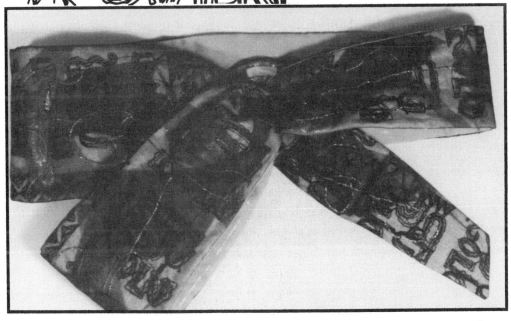

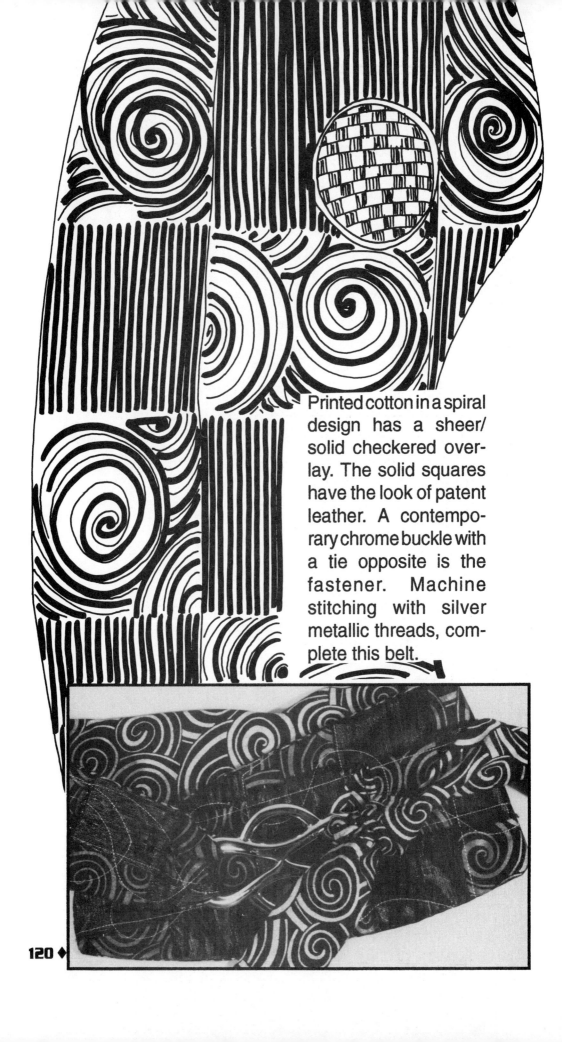

Printed cotton in a spiral design has a sheer/solid checkered overlay. The solid squares have the look of patent leather. A contemporary chrome buckle with a tie opposite is the fastener. Machine stitching with silver metallic threads, complete this belt.

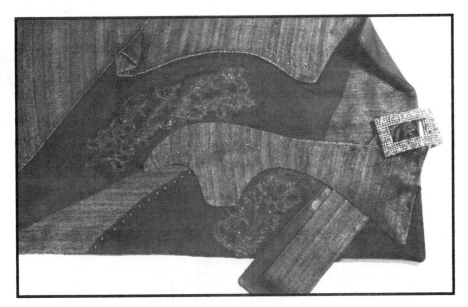

Antique beaded pieces with cut steel beads were the starting point for this belt. The beaded sections are covered with silk organza to protect them from wear. Charcoal silk tussah shapes are faced with muted grey stripes and sewn to an underlining. A non-functional cut steel buckle adorns the center front. This wide belt is shaped to start near the waist and extend to the hips in a peplum fashion.

To shape the belt, make darts in the underlining, keep doing it all around until the fabric fits the body. Then cover the shaped underlining with the fabric and embellishment of your choice.

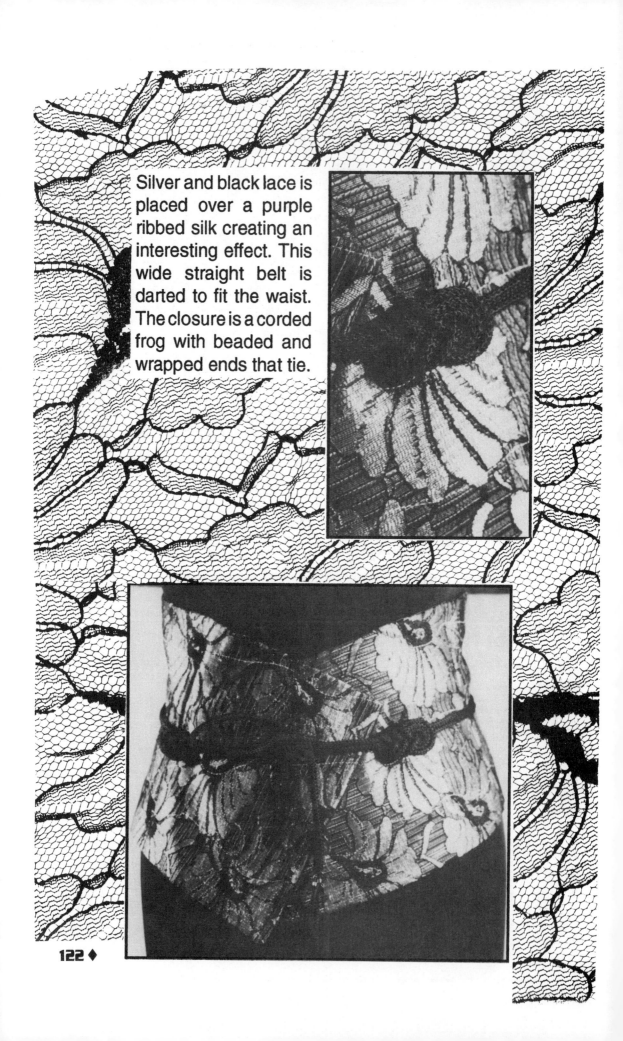

Silver and black lace is placed over a purple ribbed silk creating an interesting effect. This wide straight belt is darted to fit the waist. The closure is a corded frog with beaded and wrapped ends that tie.

This is a very wide peplum shaped 'wrap' belt that covers the hips. Leaf shapes are cut of handpainted fabric and organza in several colors. Machine stitching accents the leaves. The leaves are placed on hand-woven cotton with bias tubes to simulate stems. All is covered with ivory silk organza.

The 3-D leaves are faced shapes combining the painted fabric with the sheers. Frosted glass buttons accentuate the design and relate to the hazy look of the organza.

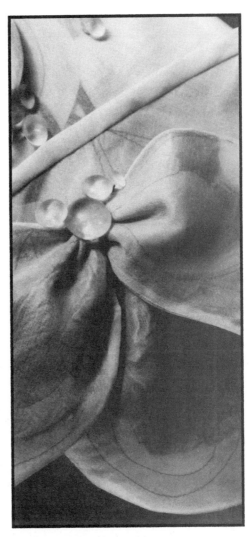

leather

Leather is available in many weights and textures. Garment weight smooth leather or suede is easily stitched and can be combined with fabric effectively.

Leather scraps are reasonably priced and usually available by the pound in leather supply stores.

Leather stretches so some adhesive is needed to keep the leather shapes in place. To apply leather pieces use glue stick for a temporary hold. For a more permanent adhesive use Barge Cement or a light coating of a spray on glue.

Stitch the leather shapes in place using a fairly long stitch so the stitching doesn't tear the leather. Also it is recommended that Singer Yellow Band needles (on any machine) be used to avoid skipped stitches.

Leather dyes or paints are available where leather products are sold if you wish to embellish the leather further.

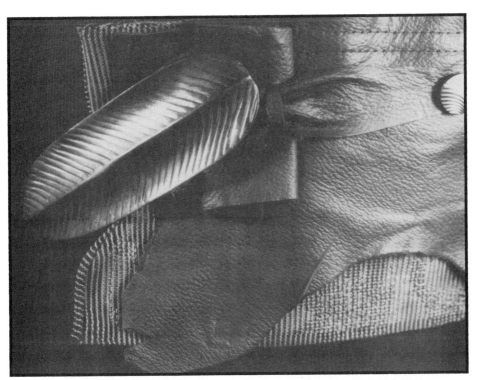

Burgundy leather is combined with copper fabric from an old obi from Japan. Stitching with copper metallic thread emphasizes the lines on the fabric and relates to the copper buttons and buckle. The natural edges of the leather are creatively used to enhance the design of the belt.

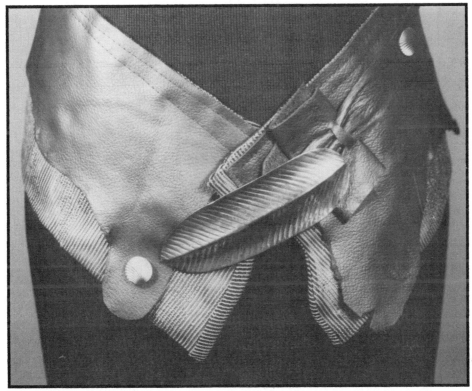

Teal green leather is cut taking advantage of the shape of the edges of the leather. The top folds over to fit the waist and to make it slightly narrower. The long bone beads are applied with narrow strips of the leather. The closure is a gold colored metal buckle with a bone inset.

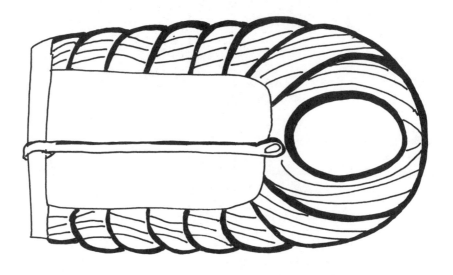

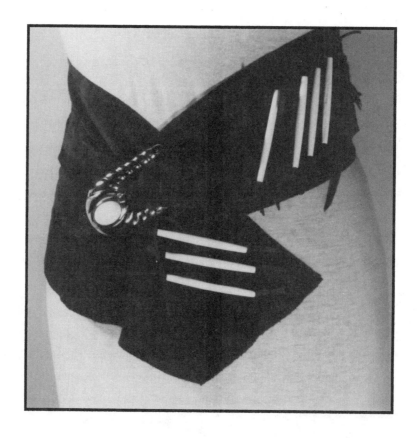

Large black leather pieces take advantage of naturally shaped edges. Taupe leather scraps are stitched in place. Two long slits are cut on the left side to create an opening. The right side of the belt slides thru the opening; the weight and length of it keeps it in place.

discharge

Most dark colored cottons have been dyed over natural or base colors. Therefore, the dark color can be removed by bleaching.

Caution: Bleach is toxic so use outside or in a well ventilated room.

Method to discharge: Use a mixture of 1/2 bleach and 1/2 water. You may wish to experiment and try less bleach, 1/3 to 2/3's water. This mixture can be brushed on, sprayed on, sponged on or ?.... just get it on!

Before you start, prepare three buckets; two with plain water and one with 1 qt. white vinegar and 3 qts. water. The vinegar solution neutralizes the bleach.

It's best to discharge small pieces since the bleach can weaken the fibers when left on too long. I do pieces that are 2 yds. or less.

Suggestion:
... try a small scrap first to reveal the underlying color. You may have to try quite a few fabrics to find one that is right for you. (Often black fabrics are dyed over brown).

Note: The bleach will have different effects if the fabric is wet, dry, wrinkled, pre-washed or not pre-washed (sizing still in it).

The bleaching action starts immediately so when the desired effect has been reached put fabric in water, then vinegar/water, then water again, wringing after each dip.

When all the pieces are rinsed, machine wash with soap or detergent, thru one wash cycle.

When the 'under' color is white or light, paint or dye can be applied to those areas, if desired. Permanent markers are effective.

(Thanks to Janet Pray for this technique)

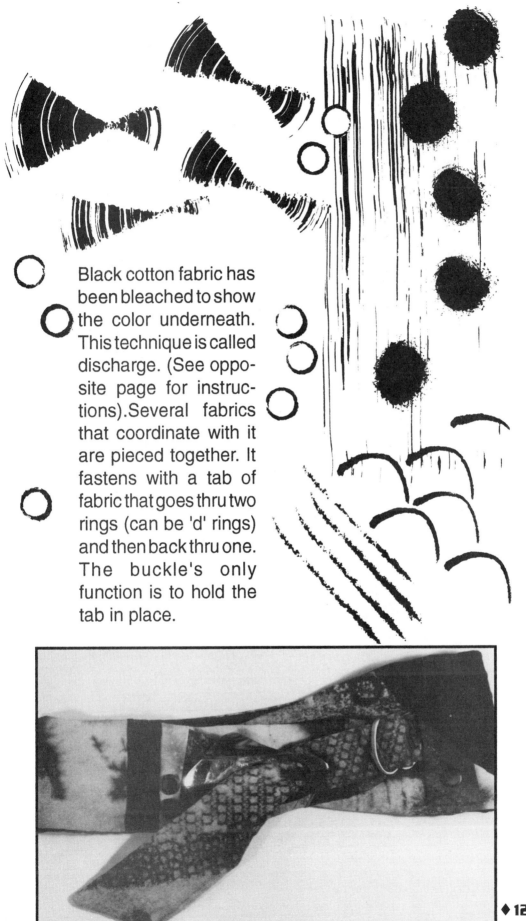

Black cotton fabric has been bleached to show the color underneath. This technique is called discharge. (See opposite page for instructions).Several fabrics that coordinate with it are pieced together. It fastens with a tab of fabric that goes thru two rings (can be 'd' rings) and then back thru one. The buckle's only function is to hold the tab in place.

Tools & Supplies

Some of the tools and supplies listed are ones that are necessary, others would just be nice to have to make our work easier.

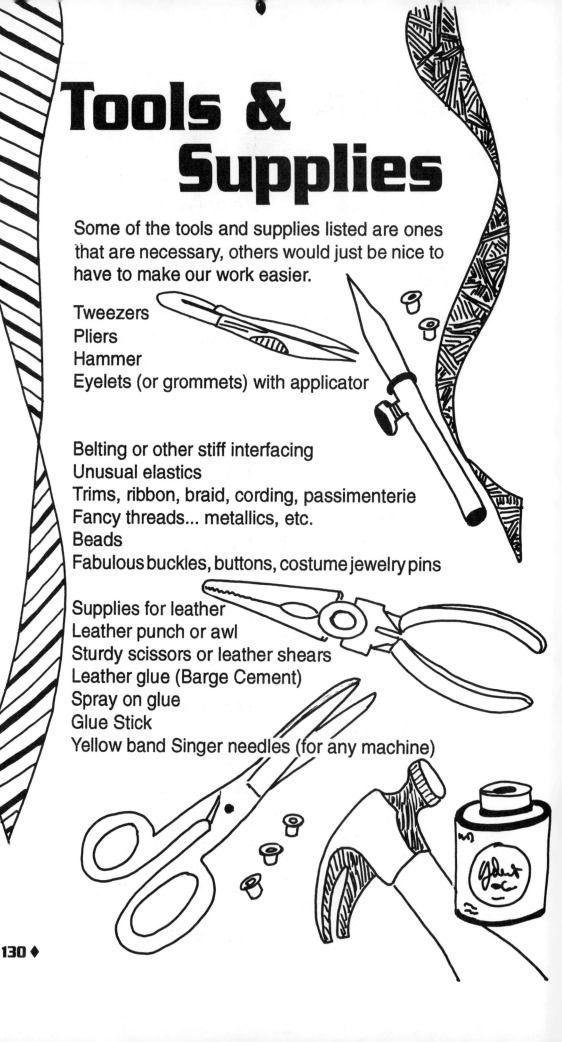

Tweezers
Pliers
Hammer
Eyelets (or grommets) with applicator

Belting or other stiff interfacing
Unusual elastics
Trims, ribbon, braid, cording, passimenterie
Fancy threads... metallics, etc.
Beads
Fabulous buckles, buttons, costume jewelry pins

Supplies for leather
Leather punch or awl
Sturdy scissors or leather shears
Leather glue (Barge Cement)
Spray on glue
Glue Stick
Yellow band Singer needles (for any machine)

Index

a

antique embroidery, 62, 63

b

basics, 6-15
beads, 44, 57, 67, 75, 85, 87, 103, 110, 117, 126
bias, 42, 81, 107, 108, 110, 123
bracelets, 9, 38, 80, 87, 96, 109, 119
braid, 53, 57, 105, 116
braided strips, 59
brass fasteners, 42, 114, 115
buckles, 8, 33, 41, 44, 45, 48, 49, 52, 53, 56, 61, 66, 74, 75, 83, 91, 93, 94, 118, 120, 121,125,126,129
buttons 52, 65, 96, 97, 98, 99, 101, 102, 104, 108, 116, 123, 125

c

chains, 46, 54, 55
chatelaine, 56
checks, 105, 120
closures, 35-49
collage, 42, 112, 114, 115
container, 56
cording, 47, 64, 85, 101, 110, 111
creativity, 5, 69

d

darts, 11
discharge, 128, 129
drawer pull, 103

e

elastic, 40, 49
embellishment, 51-67
eyelets, 93

f

fabric choices, 8
faced shapes, 87, 92-99, 121
free-motion stitching, 73
frog, 36, 122

Design Worksheet

Stop... before you close the book! Why not take a minute, right now to note some ideas?

Design Worksheet

How about developing a theme in a series?

Design Worksheet

What would happen if you started with one concept and expanded on it many times?

Design Worksheet

Brilliant thoughts......

Design Worksheet

Where would images from nature or architecture lead you?

Design Worksheet

Design closures... possibly a new way to use ordinary objects.

Design Worksheet

New shapes for a belt.....

Design Worksheet

Does it have to be a belt? Certainly not! Many ideas are coming from your experimenting, so what other concepts are possible?

Author

What a joy to have a job that I love... to look forward to it with anticipation. The less I separate my work from my personal life the happier I am.

I enjoy teaching...being with others who share the same love of sewing.
I enjoy writing... a way to share what I know with those who have the same interests.
I enjoy being in my studio ... my special place where everything is all right... to share a passion for my work with myself — my only competitor.

Lois

Order Form

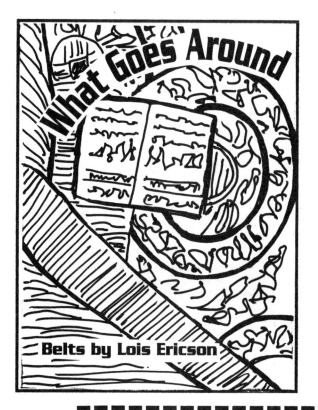

Belts by Lois Ericson

WHAT GOES AROUND

I have made more than 60 belts to inspire you to add this fashion accessory to your wardrobe. There are 144 pages, full of pictures and illustrations to assist you in creating wonderful belts for you, for gifts, or for sale. $18.

ERIC'S PRESS ORDER FORM TO:
LOIS ERICSON, BOX 5222, SALEM OR 97304

quantity	title	price	amount
	THE GREAT PUT ON	$20.	
	WHAT GOES AROUND	$18.	
	BELT PATTERN	$10.	
	SUBSCRIPTION – GOOD NEWS RAG ...... FOR CANADIAN CUSTOMERS	$ 8. $10.	
		TOTAL	

P&H for individual orders $3.00 for 1-3 books, .50 each additional

Name _____

Address _____

City, St. & Zip _____

Please send workshop information ☐

..... Comes Around